Fairhaven:
God's Mighty Oak

The Development
of the Fairhaven Ministry
The First Three Decades
Volume I

Carroll J. Olm, D.D.

Printed in United States of America

PINE HILL PRESS, INC.
Freeman, S. Dak.   57029

To the memory of —

the Rev. Paul A. Olm and Hulda J. P. Olm,

who nurtured their three children

in the faith!

Table of Contents

Dietitian Constance Hornickel
Dietition Mary Lynn Mason
Directors of Nursing
Dorothy Bell
Successor Directors of Nursing
Lillian Cahill and Olive Crawley
Directors of Activities
Loa Hill and Wendy Lucht
Directors of Social Service
Ann Ahlman
Valerie Cole and Kay Demler
Administration
Margaret Winch and Ella Brigham
Doris Germundson
Shirley Hansen
Non-Department Head Employees
Longevity
Staff Consultants
Medical Directors
Recruiting Physicians
Medical Doctors on the Board of Directors
Volunteers
The Olm Family

Foreword

Months before my retirement [January 1, 1990], and for several years after my retirement, members of the Fairhaven family [directors, staff members and residents] urged me to write a history of Fairhaven. This was echoed by church and community leaders.

The idea of putting the Fairhaven story on paper intrigued me, but nothing was done about it through March 1995. Other worthy commitments took precedence.

In April 1995, while I was rehabilitating from hip replacement surgery, our daughter, Elizabeth Eberhardt of Perrysburg, Ohio, kindly but emphatically chastised me to "get going" on the Fairhaven story. Without Beth's "forty lashes of the wet noodle," I probably would have procrastinated longer, maybe forever!

Working through the preparation of Volume I was a pleasant experience. Doing the research brought back many fond and some not so fond, memories. The writing was spasmodic! When the Spirit inspired, pages and pages were written. But there were "dry spells" when the "work" lay dormant with no progress, even for a month or two. Parts were written in the west, in the south, in Europe and in the Holy Land, but most of the writing was done in Whitewater. Through God's grace it has come together!

Preface

FAIRHAVEN: GOD'S MIGHTY OAK — [The Development of the Fairhaven Ministry — The First Three Decades] will be printed in two volumes. The first volume, which follows, is **not** strictly a chronological, historical sequence of what transpired. The various chapters are topical themes which, in the main, reflect events occurring from the 1950's until the year 1963. Great liberty was taken in several chapters, especially the chapters on "The Staff" and "Oldster Funny Bones," to include what happened through the three decades, until January 1, 1990, the date of my retirement.

To adequately describe the Fairhaven ministry, it was necessary to go far beyond simple citing of historical fact. Effort was made to include the "why" of actions, the stories behind the story, the motivations, the philosophy, the theology and testimony to the faith. Long quotations are included to reflect the abstract, an attempt to convey the heart, the spirit of Fairhaven, which had to be developed.

The second volume will include a chronological, year by year, account of the continuing life of Fairhaven from 1963 to 1990. It will include personal reflections on events which occurred , a "lifting up" of significant leadership contributions by board members and others who served during those years, and testimony to the faith upon which the entire ministry is based.

It is my hope and prayer that no persons will be offended in any way, should there be unintentional omissions or if greater emphasis should have been given to certain events, persons or areas of discussion. The magnitude of the Fairhaven ministry is truly significant — and the task to compile material, summarize multifaceted and interlocking movements, and to capture the spirit of the development has been a challenge.

Fairhaven belongs to God and to God must be the glory! If this is conveyed in the writing, then, though everything else be a failure, all the time and effort has been worthwhile.

Acknowledgements

I am indebted to Thomas S. McLeRoy, Whitewater, Wisconsin,

William J. Willis, Anna Maria, Florida,

and Frederick R. Trost, Madison, Wisconsin [Chapter XI],

for editing copy and for providing helpful suggestions.

Also, to Jack G. Trojan, Whitewater, Wisconsin,

for title improvement.

A big debt of gratitude to Marilyn G. Olm [Mrs. Wonderful]

for being my "sounding board" and for her continuing

encouragement.

The Oaks—1963

CHAPTER I

The Oaks

"God looked at what [was done]. All of it was very good."
Genesis 1:31

Two large burr oak trees stand erect on the front lawns of the Fairhaven grounds. They are long standing, majestic, beautiful and over the years have harbored squirrels, chipmunks, at least one raccoon, one peacock, an owl, and sundry species of smaller birds — a haven for many of God's creatures. These burr oaks symbolize the Fairhaven ministry! They symbolize continuity, strength, security, beauty! Through the years they survived all adverse elements: lightning and thunder storms, severe winters, hot and arid summers, sweeping winds, and tornadoes. They also survived those well meaning, but shortsighted, construction people who wanted to cut them down so building erection would be less difficult. After decades, these burr oaks still stand proudly at Fairhaven's side. One can almost hear them saying,

"Fairhaven, you have grown up within our shadows and you, Fairhaven, are so much like us —

You are strong and majestic!
You are lasting and beautiful!
You have survived the snows and the winds!
You are a haven for God's loved ones!

Yes, Fairhaven, God has nurtured us! Through God's grace we have grown from acorns into oaks."

CHAPTER II

The Fairhaven Acorn

". . . . .I will never leave [you,] nor forsake[you.]"
Hebrews 13:5, KJV

In God's plan for the universe an acorn is needed before an oak tree can grow! For Fairhaven the Rev. Dr. Jess H. Norenberg was that acorn! He rightfully is called "the FATHER of FAIRHAVEN." He had served as the superintendent of the Wisconsin Congregational Conference from 1948 until 1962 when the Wisconsin Congregational churches united with the North and South Wisconsin synods of the Evangelical and Reformed Church to become the Wisconsin Conference of the United Church of Christ. Everyone called him "Jess" for there was little pretentiousness about him, and he wanted people to accept him as he was.

Most acquaintances liked him and were delighted with his lovely wife, Loretta. Together they traveled the state, coordinating the ministries and missions of the Congregationalists of Wisconsin.

Jess Norenberg was a preacher, teacher, campaigner, builder, loving spouse, fond father and certainly a friend to all. He was an "example setter." Never did he ask another to do what he himself would not do. Although hundreds were involved in the development of Fairhaven, it was Jess Norenberg who was the prime mover and the guiding hand. He gave his strength, his talent and his money to make Fairhaven a success. Jess was the "Father of Fairhaven!"

For nearly a decade, the lay members [and ministers, too] of the Wisconsin Congregational Conference had wanted to do something for older people. There was continuing talk at association and conference meetings and elsewhere about the possibility of having the conference build a home for the aging in Wisconsin. Nothing materialized from this talk. It was only after Jess Norenberg made a personal commitment to dedicate his time and leadership to this vision that anything happened. When he spearheaded the drive to build a Congregational home, much support was generated.

Jess knew that there were significant numbers of Congregational members who wanted to see a home for the aging materialize and who were willing to devote time, talent and money toward such a project. The desire was there! What was needed was to have the most respected leader of the conference declare that the organization and implementa-

3

tion of such a project was not only possible, but doable and desirable. Not unanimously, but certainly to a great extent, when Jess projected this program, Congregationalists responded affirmatively. Individuals loved and respected Jess and translated that love and respect into support. Jess was an eloquent speaker and used this eloquence to drive home his points. He also had political savvy and knew how to get "ducks in line" before key votes were taken. While conference superintendents had little power, Jess effectively utilized covenant relationships to accomplish his goals. Without this gifted leader, what was later to be known as "Fairhaven" would never have been accomplished.

Jess H. Norenberg—1972

On May 11, 1953, at Antigo, Wisconsin, the Wisconsin Congregational Conference Board of Directors voted a three fold proposal:

    a.   To appoint a committee to aggressively explore the possibilities of such a home.
    b.   To begin to accumulate funds for such a home.
    c.   To provide guidelines for Congregational attorneys in the state, urging them to suggest bequests to such a home when assisting clients in the preparation of their wills.

Two years later, on May 9, 1955, the Wisconsin Congregational Conference Board of Directors reviewed a proposed constitution and bylaws for a community for the aging. They thoroughly evaluated the document. Attorney William Bradford Smith, a member of First Congregational Church, Madison, Wisconsin, devoted much time and energy to this endeavor.

In Superintendent Jess Norenberg's written report to the 117th Annual Meeting of the Wisconsin Congregational Conference [May 10-12, 1955] at First Congregational Church, Wisconsin Rapids, Wisconsin, he referred to the "Community for the Aging":

Whenever this project is presented it awakens both interest and enthusiasm. Already it has taken days of my time, days well spent if thereby we can bring into service a community where older people may spend their sunset years. Details and arrangements await your decisions. This will be your home and you must decide the conditions under which guests will be accepted. It is my conviction that the home should be operated under a special corporation and that we should plan on about 150 guests, a percentage of these to be ministers and their wives.

Upon recommendation from the Conference Board of Directors, the following resolution was adopted at the 117th Annual Meeting of the Wisconsin Congregational Conference [May 10-12, 1955] at First Congregational Church, Wisconsin Rapids, Wisconsin, with a vote of 328 to 1:

We therefore move that as a preliminary condition to operating a "Community for the Aging" at Eau Claire, Wisconsin, the Wisconsin Congregational Conference raise $100,000 cash by May 1956 to be used as working capital, and that each congregation be asked to raise a minimum sum equal to 10% of its 1954 home expense budget as published in the 1954 year book; that the acceptance of these goals be reported not later than the fall association meetings in 1955; that the executive committee is to cooperate with the conference office and other churches toward these ends.

In the summer of 1955, much excitement arose when Mr. Henry Ingram offered to the Wisconsin Congregational Conference the E. B. Ingram estate near Eau Claire, Wisconsin. He wanted it to be used for a Community for the Aging. The estate embraced a residence building and scenic acreage. However, on August 29, 1955, Mr. Ingram withdrew his offer, based upon his better understanding the program direction. Harvey Sherwood wrote, "The offer was so limited that development of the facility looked almost impossible. So, the 'bubble' of our hope was suddenly punctured."

The derailment of the Ingram/Eau Claire plans had its effect on the conference and its constituency. Nothing toward the goal of having a "community for the aging" materialized during the next two years.

Then, in anticipation of the May 13-15, 1958, Annual Meeting of the Wisconsin Congregational Conference at Second Congregational Church, Beloit, Wisconsin, Superintendent Norenberg included in his report to

the conference membership the following paragraph under the title
"Senior Citizens":

> A few years ago we ventured boldly into the field of Christian
> care for the aging. At that time it seemed that the costs would be
> borne largely by others. Let us again tackle this opportunity with
> the understanding that what we will do will need to be paid for
> by us.

Undoubtedly, this put a new "twist" on the project. Nothing of
progress was made at the 1958 Annual Meeting of the Conference.

By March 20, 1959, the Wisconsin Congregational Conference Board
of Directors had considered various types of programming and buildings
for the projected community for the aging. Lay leaders, such as Dr. O. J.
Gates and Attorney Thorpe Merriman of Fort Atkinson, Wisconsin, and
Harold Brandenburg of Madison, Wisconsin, were involved.

Since a site was imperative, Jess turned his attention to property
acquisition for conference purposes. *Congregational Church Life,* the
monthly communication vehicle of the conference, was used to encourage Congregationalists across the state to send "site suggestions" to the
conference office. Response was gratifying and all suggested sites were
investigated by the conference leaders. None seemed more suitable for
conference purposes than the one suggested by long standing
Congregationalist Viola Humphrey of Whitewater, Wisconsin, who submitted a Whitewater site through her pastor, the Rev. Donald S. Hobbs.
Details in regard to the Whitewater site are included in Chapter VII —
"The Site and the Buildings."

On May 11, 1959, the conference board of directors went on record
favoring acquisition of the Whitewater site for a home for the aging and
favoring the purchase of the property.

Dr. Norenberg reported to the conference membership in advance of
the 121st Annual Meeting of the Wisconsin Congregational Conference
[May 12-14, 1959], First Congregational Church, Madison, Wisconsin, as
follows:

> The Board of Directors continues to wrestle with this matter.
> No longer is the question of need, but there is wide divergence on
> where, and when, and how? At least five patterns suggest them-
> selves: dormitory living as in Plymouth Place, La Grange, Illinois;
> cottage living as in Pilgrim Place in California; apartment living
> as in Mayflower Home, Iowa; a series of small homes scattered
> over the state as Presbyterian Homes in Pennsylvania; and a

combination of two or more of these patterns. We cannot be excused for further delay. Steps should be taken immediately to select a plan and a place. And, unless anyone be tempted to make small plans, let us think of $100,000 a year for each of the next ten years.

Authorization to purchase the Whitewater property, contingent upon securing proper zoning, and to create a committee to prepare plans for a home for the aging was passed by the board of directors on October 5, 1959, in Madison, Wisconsin. The committee appointees were:

Architect:	Arthur E. Waterman, Waterman & Fuge, Fort Atkinson, Wisconsin.
Building Committee:	Ned Sperry, Fort Atkinson.
	Roswell Groves, Milwaukee, Wisconsin.
	[Later replaced by John Glaettli, Jr., Madison, Wisconsin.]
	William Bradford Smith, Madison, Wisconsin.
Furnishings: [Appointed later.]	
	Evelyn Gustafson, Fort Atkinson, Wisconsin.
	Irene Leffingwell, Whitewater, Wisconsin.
Legal Counsel:	William Bradford Smith, Madison, Wisconsin.
	Thorpe Merriman, Fort Atkinson, Wisconsin.
	William Rogers, Fort Atkinson, Wisconsin.
	William J. Willis, Milwaukee, Wisconsin.

Gradually momentum was building. It resulted in the Wisconsin Congregational Conference in annual meeting on May 10-12, 1960, at First Congregational Church, Eau Claire, Wisconsin, authorizing the conference board of directors to proceed with the erection of a home. Authorization was also given to sign the necessary contracts, borrow the necessary funds, and employ staff.

In preparation for that annual meeting, Superintendent Norenberg reported:

Whitewater is a name that has assumed new dimensions in our thinking for at our last annual meeting you instructed the Board of Directors "to purchase a site suitable for the construction of a home for the retiring." After diligent search, seven and one-half acres were purchased in Whitewater for $20,000 and an adjoining house was also acquired for $27,000. Those who inspected it claim that the site is ideal and it has been approved by the Federal Housing Authority. The Sperry committee has been busy with architects and in the exhibit room you will see drawings of possibilities. As we move forward two things should be kept in mind: in view of rising costs little dreams will be expensive, and all charity is made possible by gifts. Those who have been closest to this project believe that as far as possible we should serve the needy. Contributions will determine the degree.

On June 26, 1960, at Madison, Wisconsin, the Fairhaven Corporation articles and bylaws, authored by Attorney William Bradford Smith, were filed with the Wisconsin Secretary of State.

In 1961, Thorpe Merriman, newly elected president of the Fairhaven Board of Directors, and Conference Superintendent Jess Norenberg made two appeals to the conference constituency. Under the title "Fairhaven, Our Home In Whitewater," Mr. Merriman said:

Whereas, the Wisconsin Congregational Conference meeting in May 1960 at Eau Claire, approved the construction of Fairhaven, a home for the retiring at Whitewater;

Whereas, the board of directors has selected an administrator-chaplain, who has been on the job since January 1961;

Whereas, Fairhaven is at present the only home for the retiring specifically serving Wisconsin Congregationalists; therefore,

We urge direct action by churches and individuals to finish the work we have started;

To support Fairhaven not only by individual and collective investment, but also by writing gifts into their budgets and bequests into their wills for Fairhaven;

We recommend the formation of a Fairhaven committee in each association, to work closely with a similar committee in each church, not only to promote financial support for Fairhaven, but also to find desirable and deserving folk for residence in Fairhaven.

We further urge vigorous action immediately to get the project built, paid for, occupied and adequately supported for as long as may be necessary.

Dr. Norenberg reported:

Fairhaven continues to be a thrilling project even though progress has been retarded. We were babes in the woods when we dreamed that a substantial government loan could be negotiated overnight. The same slow pace is rather evident in the support received from the churches.

Two years ago in a meeting, by unanimous vote the Board of Directors was authorized to buy property. Last year, by the same vote, the Board was authorized to hire, borrow and get on with construction. Unfortunately ballots do not buy bricks or lay up walls. To date not more than half of our churches have put their hands to this task. Thrilling is the response of our senior citizens to the prospect of residence in this community of retirement apartments. If only each person reading this report could talk to a few of them, a fire would indeed be kindled.

The conference membership responded affirmatively to the two appeals at the 123rd Annual Meeting [May 9-11, 1961] at Green Bay, Wisconsin, by adopting two short resolutions:

The first resolution [lifted from the 123rd Annual Meeting minutes] was recorded as follows:

Borrow up to $300,000 on notes for one year at interest not to exceed 6%, renewable for one additional year, to finance Fairhaven.

The second resolution recording was:

A resolution whereby the conference out of its anticipated gifts from churches and individuals, from the surplus in annual operations, and from sums anticipated in gifts and bequests, guarantee the payment of annual deficits in Fairhaven operations, providing there are deficits.

Wisconsin Congregationalists historically had supported thrusts for higher education. Institutions such as Beloit College, Beloit, Wisconsin; Northland College, Ashland, Wisconsin; and Ripon College, Ripon, Wisconsin, were given birth through Congregational initiative. However, until the advent of Fairhaven, no Wisconsin direct service projects in Health and Human Service ministries were developed under the auspices of Congregationalism. On the other hand, the Evangelical and Reformed churches in Wisconsin had a long heritage in Health and Human Service projects. Notable among these were: Winnebago Children's Home [now Sunburst Youth Homes, Inc.,] Neillsville, Wisconsin; Evangelical Deaconess Hospital [now Sinai Samaritan Medical Center,] Milwaukee, Wisconsin; Cedar Lake Old Folks Home [now Cedar Campuses,] West Bend, Wisconsin. Another Evangelical and Reformed agency, the New Glarus Home for the Aged [now New Glarus Home, Inc.,] New Glarus, Wisconsin, was founded in 1966, shortly after Fairhaven Corporation. In addition, the Evangelical and Reformed synods were supporting Bensenville Home Society [now Lifelink, Inc.,] Bensenville, Illinois; Fort Wayne Children's Home [now Crossroad, Inc.,] Fort Wayne, Indiana; and Emmaus Homes, Inc. [serving the mentally handicapped,] St. Charles and Marthasville, Missouri.

Jess' dream was to bring into the merger of the Wisconsin Congregational churches and the North and South Evangelical and Reformed synods of Wisconsin a significant ministry to, for and with older citizens. This ministry was specifically a proposal from the Congregational side of the merger. Since the project [later to be known as Fairhaven] was to be initially larger than any previous Health and Human Service thrust from any of the three jurisdictions historically, the initiative was indeed significant.

While the merger nationally and symbolically took place in Cleveland, Ohio, in 1957, the consummation of that same merger for Wisconsin churches was not to be realized until October 26, 1962. The forthcoming merger surely placed pressure on Dr. Norenberg. It was originally conceived that the Wisconsin Congregational Conference project should be constructed and in operation by the advent of the Wisconsin Conference of the United Church of Christ. Since the Fairhaven project encountered many obstacles early in its developmental stages, the "Congregational" home entered the merger not being a completed entity.

Fairhaven construction commenced January 8, 1962. The architect established May 10, 1963, as the conclusion of construction date. On October 26, 1962, midway through construction, Fairhaven's source of birth, the Wisconsin Congregational Conference, voluntarily gave up its identity to become part of a larger and better whole, the Wisconsin Conference of the United Church of Christ.

Between May 6, 1960, [project authorization date] and October 26, 1962, Jess Norenberg addressed significant steps in the development process:

Obtaining a site.
Engaging an architect.
Engaging a manager.
Developing building plans.
Negotiating building contracts.
Searching for financing.
Promoting fund raising.
Finalizing legal matters.

True, Jess had considerable help from others for most of these steps. The Rev. Richard Wichlei, Madison, Wisconsin, Assistant Conference Superintendent [later the Southwest Association Minister of the Wisconsin Conference of the United Church of Christ], is "lifted up" as one of those helpers, along with many other lay and clergy Congregationalists. However, Jess did the coordinating and was the driving force.

In 1972, Jess Norenberg was awarded the Council for Health and Human Service Ministries Honor Award for Meritorious Service. Earlier, the Fairhaven library had been dedicated to his honor. This duly recognized his momentous contribution to Fairhaven and the Church. It must have been with great personal satisfaction that Dr. Norenberg wrote his last report to the conference membership, in anticipation of the 124th and final Annual Meeting of the Wisconsin Congregational Conference [May 8-10, 1962] at First Congregational Church, Janesville, Wisconsin. After all the delays, after all the frustrations, after years of personal dedication and sacrifice, he could write a positive report:

Fairhaven — after years of reversals, goes forward rapidly. The experts who have studied our plans are unanimous in the opinion that we are creating something fine, and that we are getting a lot for our money. The conviction grows that the Lord led us both to our architect and to our administrator-chaplain. While we are getting much for our money we are experiencing some difficulties in getting the money. As stated in last year's report, you have supported us with your ballots but your dollars are required. Unfortunately this is the first time in its 124 years that the Conference has ever voted to take a large "bite." Consequently, it may be excused for being a bit timid.

The Fairhaven acorn had sprung roots!

CHAPTER III

The Concept

"This is the Lord's doing; it is marvelous in our eyes."
Psalm 118:23, KJV

The Wisconsin Congregational Conference accepted the Fairhaven project as the conference's major mission thrust, even though the final definition was yet to be developed. The conference membership simply wanted to sponsor a retirement home for older Americans, with specific opportunity for Congregationalists themselves to make use of the project as a place for their own personal retirement. Just what kind of facility it would eventually become, what type services would or would not be offered, were questions not initially addressed. It is fair to say that many Congregationalists had visions of a facility that provided independent living units with very limited service available. The vision embraced residents coming and going freely, apartments where residents could bring their own furniture, kitchenettes for food preparation and a congenial Christian atmosphere. Residents would be freed from the burdens of maintenance — no lawn mowing, no snow shoveling, no putting on or taking off storm windows or screens. Later various services were added — housekeeping, laundry, food service, nursing service, etc. Eventually, Fairhaven provided all components of care and was nationally recognized for its service quality. Originally, a Fairhaven skilled nursing unit [infirmary] was projected for five years after the first residential construction.

Residency, not institutionalism, was the by-word. It is quite remarkable and much to the credit and faith of the Wisconsin Congregationalists that they not only accepted the general, undefined concept, but also gave loyal support toward its culmination. A publicity brochure, printed years later, gave some definition to what was implemented as basic concept:

FAIRHAVEN
Where Life Is Added To Years
IF YOU
... wish to be free from the burden of
caring for your home...
... seek sociability and yet want
privacy respected...

13

. . . want to live independently with
freedom to come and go. . .
. . . desire to position yourself for care
priority. . .
T H E N
FAIRHAVEN At Whitewater
is for you!

Early in 1961 a small group of conference leaders — including Jess H. Norenberg, Dr. O.J. Gates, Thorpe Merriman and the new administrator-chaplain — drove to Grinnell, Iowa, to visit The Mayflower Home. This facility was operating under the auspices of the Iowa Congregational Conference and was the closest in concept to the residential living projections that were being formulated by the Wisconsin Congregational Conference for its future facility. Retirement homes of this type, where older people could live in independent apartments, were rapidly appearing in California, where the concept really became instantly very popular. At that time there were no such facilities in the State of Wisconsin and only The Mayflower Home at Grinnell in the Midwest. Plymouth Place of LaGrange, Illinois, had made its significant contribution, but was more transitional in nature, attempting to blend the Old Folks Home philosophy of yesteryear with the newer residential thrusts. The group visiting Grinnell saw a short 80 plus year old resident struggling to iron her bed sheets on an ironing board. Immediately, a commitment was made to provide flat laundry services at the future Fairhaven.

Ministries to and for older people existing in the Midwest were steeped in the quasi medical mold of the nursing home. The facilities had identical in size institutional type smaller rooms, with furniture identical in all units and in most cases bath rooms shared. These typical "Old Folks Homes" were linked with nursing sections where excellent care was provided. Some had constructed new buildings to accommodate this philosophical approach to care, but they had not "broken out" of the traditional modes. These homes provided excellent service and were successful operations. Among the more noted not-for-profit facilities in southeastern Wisconsin [in 1960-61] were Cedar Lake Home for the Aged, West Bend; Home for Aged Lutherans, Wauwatosa; Luther Manor, Wauwatosa; Methodist Manor, West Allis; Milwaukee Catholic Home, Milwaukee; Milwaukee Jewish Home, Milwaukee; Protestant Home for the Aged, Milwaukee; and St. John's Episcopal Home, Milwaukee.

All of the administrators of these facilities were visited in 1961 by the new administrator-chaplain of Fairhaven. The Fairhaven residential, apartment type, concept was shared as the thrust the Wisconsin Congregational Conference was projecting. In every case — with no exceptions — the administrators rejected the Fairhaven concept and suggested that a nursing home be built. It was somewhat disconcerting to hear these negative reactions to what the Wisconsin Congregational Conference had conceived as a needed, innovative, and satisfying concept for older citizens. However, these reactions did not change the commitment to have a retirement facility and not an institutional old folks home — nursing home — constructed. The Fairhaven leadership was not discouraged, believing the projected thrust was on the "cutting edge" of new programming for seniors. The Fairhaven leaders were resolute in their commitment to make a success of the project. Two benefits were derived from the interviews: 1] Fairhaven would need to direct continuous, positive publicity to the churches and the general public to make it easier for those new to the concept to accept the innovation. 2] Provision for skilled nursing beds might be needed before the five year projection as originally conceived.

Administration could not wait the five years to address nursing care. This issue had to be resolved immediately. The board of directors resolved it by creating an initial 21 bed infirmary [skilled nursing section.] Residency rather than institutionalism, yes, but residency that offered a continuous care program with monthly rates increasing proportionate to the care required.

Fairhaven was the first Wisconsin retirement home to provide apartments with kitchenettes, the first to offer different sized units where the resident provided his/her own furniture, the first to allow the residents' pictures to be hung on the walls and to provide a continuum of care until hospitalization.

[Twenty years later, every one of the facilities visited had developed the residential, apartment type, services as part of their programs. Thus they embraced the Fairhaven concept and provided wider dimension and greater enhancement for their ministries.]

THE MOTTO

At the very first meeting of the Fairhaven Board of Directors, the administrator-chaplain introduced what became the Fairhaven motto — "Where Life Is Added To Years." This motto symbolized what the ministry was conceived to be. It was to be a place of life, of living, of enrichment, of growth. In the words of Genevieve Spradling, an 80 year Sparta Congregationalist, "I could go to the Old Folks Home near here or to the County Home, but I am not ready to sit down, put my hands in my lap and wait to die. I long for a place where I can come and go freely, where I am released from the burden of house maintenance, but where I may also bring my own furniture and put my own pictures on the walls, where I can still bake my own cookies whenever I want. Thank God for Fairhaven!"

The motto captivated people. After participating in an annual meeting of the Wisconsin Conference of the United Church of Christ, Marilyn Olm shared that two persons, on separate occasions, initiated conversation about the motto with her.

The concept was summarized by the administrator-chaplain in early publicity vehicles as follows:

> The Christian philosophy of Fairhaven is embodied in the motto "Where Life Is Added To Years." Science has put years on life. It is the church's responsibility and Fairhaven's objective to add life to the years.
>
> To make this philosophy realistic, five major goals are being pursued.
>
> The first of these goals is to place the emphasis on residence and not on institutionalism. The buildings were constructed with this in mind. People who live at Fairhaven are not patients, inmates or numbers. They are residents, the sanctity of whose apartments is preserved as the sanctity of regular homes is preserved. The staff, residents, and visitors do not enter an apartment without permission. Staff members make exception to this only if there is suspicion of physical distress or mechanical malfunction.
>
> Older people do not like to be herded into groups any more than other people do. They want to preserve their dignity and self-respect. Fairhaven's policies allow the residents to enjoy life at its fullest. The apartment is the resident's own personal haven.
>
> Independence is the second goal — where one can come and go as one likes and even participate in part-time employment if desired. The apartment key opens any exterior door. All meals can be prepared at the kitchenette, or, if preferred, one or more can be purchased in the dining room. The residents are urged to bring their own furniture and decorate their walls with pictures and mirrors. Dwellers at Fairhaven can be completely self-sufficient or look to the home for given needs.
>
> Goal number three is continued growth. Whoever believes that older persons do not grow has not read or observed much. Some of the greatest strides in progressive thought has come from the Golden Age clubs across the country. Fairhaven's

lounges and recreational areas provide excellent opportunity for creative activities. University of Wisconsin - Whitewater works closely with the staff of Fairhaven to integrate the residents into collegiate opportunities. The site of the home is located so close to the heart of the community activities that residents can participate in the life-stream of Whitewater. If we want to normalize old age, we must give our older citizens back to the communities and stop trying to isolate them.

The fourth objective is security. Medical, emotional, financial, and spiritual security is needed — security from isolation during illness, security from maintenance problems, security from multiplicity of bills, freedom from anxieties, freedom from boredom and freedom from fear. Through the comforts and services of its program, Fairhaven meets these needs.

Fairhaven wants to be strictly Christian [the fifth objective.] It wants to demonstrate its love for the Lord and the place it has in the ministry to [God's] people. It has a chapel for meditation and prayer, devotionals, and vespers. It has a chaplain for guidance, counsel, and directed Bible study. Above all, it embraces the knowledge that everyone desires to help bear one another's burdens and so fulfill the law of Christ.

To adequately serve the needs of our people, we feel it is necessary to minister to the whole of the person. Strong bodies — yes — but just as important are strong minds, active hands and fervent spirits. Only as we meet the mental, emotional, social and spiritual needs of our people, in addition to their physical need, is "life added to years." To this end, we dedicate what we have and what we are.

The motto "Where Life Is Added To Years" was universally approved and accepted by constituents of the Fairhaven ministry. It epitomized the Fairhaven concept. Walter and Louise Buell, Sturgeon Bay, Wisconsin, realized this and were so excited and captivated by it that they purchased a large decorative stone. With board approval, the Buells attached two bronze plaques to the stone. One "lifted up" the Fairhaven motto. The other stated: "In honor of the Administrator-chaplain Carroll J. Olm." The stone was placed on the Fairhaven grounds at the Starin Road west drive entrance.

ADMINISTRATOR-CHAPLAIN TITLE

Numerous titles were considered for the new administrative head. Administrator-chaplain was chosen. It clarified the position, linking management with spiritual life, blending service with Christian dedication. Hence, from the very onset, Fairhaven was grounded in church-relatedness, making it distinctly Christian both in concept and practice. Decisions would be made taking into consideration the wholeness of the person — not only the physical, but the mental, emotional, social, spiritual aspects as well. [See Chapter XI - "Church-Relatedness".]

THE NAME: FAIRHAVEN

Fairhaven concept was epitomized not only through the motto "Where Life Is Added To Years," not only via the meaningful descriptive title "administrator-chaplain," but predominantly through its very name — "*FAIRHAVEN.*" Many persons, over the years, have said that Fairhaven could not have a better name. The name Fairhaven is Biblical [Acts 27:8,] which speaks to Christian heritage. The name is symbolic, describing basic characteristics — "fair" interpreted "pleasant" or "beautiful" — and "haven" conveying "protection" or "security."

Originator of the name was the Rev. Harvey Sherwood, Gays Mills, Wisconsin. The conference had appealed to members of all congregations to submit possible names for the soon to be facility. It was Harvey Sherwood's suggestion, made on June 22, 1960, which prevailed. By a mail ballot of the Wisconsin Congregational Conference Board of Directors, sometime prior to August 16, 1960, the name Fairhaven was approved.

The following letter, suitably preserved, was Mr. Sherwood's contribution to concept:

June 22, 1960
Dear Jess:
    I have one more suggestion for a name for the Whitewater home. It is
                        FAIR HAVENS
    This could be written as one word: "Fairhavens" or "Fairhaven."
    This name would have some biblical connection since that was one of the ports entered by the ship carrying Paul to Rome. Its meaning: "Fair" meaning beautiful; "Haven" meaning a place of shelter and safety.
    The name would be distinctive, easily spoken, and limited to the two or three syllables which you think desirable.
    If we wanted a name with Congregational flavor we could use: "Pilgrim Havens." However this is longer and doesn't "roll off the tongue" too easily.

Anyway I would like to put this name into the running. I think "haven" has a connotation which would appeal.

Cordially,

/s/ Harvey Sherwood.

HARVEY SHERWOOD

Harvey Sherwood

Harvey Sherwood was special! He was a successful Gays Mills banker who had a love for the Lord and the church. He served the Gays Mills Congregational Church as a lay minister for many years. After his pursuing theological and church-related courses, after his demonstrating effective leadership and a highly regarded life style, Harvey was licensed to administer the sacraments in the Gays Mills parish. Later that licensure was broadened, first to the geographic area of the LaCrosse Association and then to the entire State of Wisconsin. The conference ordained him and later elected him as moderator of the conference.

During Fairhaven's early development Harvey was in dual leadership capacity. He served as chair of the conference board of directors and was elected as one of the nine initial members of the Fairhaven Corporation Board of Directors. He, with his lovely wife Bertha, was an avid supporter of the cause and used every personal effort to publicize and move the program ahead. Later this special couple came to reside at Fairhaven until their respective deaths. While at Fairhaven, Harvey produced an effective filmstrip entitled "The Throw-Away Generation" that focused on the rich resources available amongst retired persons. God be praised for loaning us Christians like the Sherwoods!

FEES CONCEPT

Pursuant to Fairhaven's initial resident agreement, Fairhaven application fees of $500 would be applied on the founders fees. The founders fee was an up-front payment to the corporation for the leasing of an apartment. Founders fee charges ranged from $7,000 to $10,500 per apartment. Since the charge was made for the apartment, not per individual, two residents living together would each pay one-half. [$5,250 each for the largest $10,500 apartment.] Fairhaven retained 10% of the founders fee for each year or portion of a year of residency. Should a resident voluntarily leave, the unused portion of the founders fee would be refunded

90 days after the written notice of agreement termination was received. After nine years and one day of residency, the founders fee would be used up and there would be no refund should the agreement be terminated. Upon a resident's death, there would be no founders fee refund to the estate. [After 20 plus years of operation, it was calculated that those residents who lived beyond the ten years offset those who lived at Fairhaven less than ten years. The average residency length was 9.9 years.] Monthly maintenance fees ranging from $60 to $100 per apartment were charged to cover the cost of Fairhaven's operations. The resident received all utilities [except telephone,] flat laundry, heavy housekeeping duties, activities, counseling, spiritual ministries, use of all the common facilities and some nursing care. Food service in the dining room was at or below cost. Fairhaven was one of the very few facilities where residents were **not** forced to eat at least one meal per day in the dining room. Residents could use the dining room services per their desire. This policy made it more difficult to administer the food service department since dining room usage varied per needs or desires of the residency. The policy also made it difficult for the food service department to fiscally break even, since at times the volume was low. Nevertheless, as in all decisions made, the resident was considered first and every effort was made to preserve resident choice. Fairhaven was being operated for the residency! Its main purpose was not to achieve a strong bottom line for the corporation.

CHRISTIAN CHARITY

Christian charity was a major projection. Worthy Christians, who could not afford to pay their own way were to be considered for founders fee grants. Despite early financial difficulties, founder fee grants were given, the first being in the amounts of $5,250 and $9,000. The board of directors appointed a committee to address charitable activity potential. Director John Vergeront, attorney from Plymouth Congregational Church, Milwaukee, chaired the committee. Other members were: Theodora Klug, Menomonee Falls, the Rev. Trent Rockwell, Burlington, and E. R. Klassy, Fort Atkinson. Over the years additional founders fee grants were given. These were never publicized since board members took the position that the corporation's charitable activity should not be flaunted.

CHAPTER IV

The First Board of Directors

"Your heavenly Father is. . . . .ready to give the Holy Spirit
to anyone who asks."
Luke 11:13, KJV [paraphrased]

The initial organizational structure of the Fairhaven ministry was unique and unwieldy! Since this ministry was conference initiated, the Conference Board of Directors maintained authority over the program. At the time the Fairhaven Corporation Board of Directors nominees were elected and the administrator-chaplain was engaged, they were advised that the conference board would continue exercising jurisdiction over the project until the buildings were completed. The conference board was to be responsible for the site, the architect, fund raising, the financing and the construction. It was made clear that the Fairhaven board and administrator-chaplain were elected and engaged to operate the facility.

Authorization for the creation of an initial nine member board of directors was voted on June 9, 1960, by the executive committee of the Wisconsin Congregational Conference Board of Directors. These nine members were: Harold Brandenburg, Madison; O.J. Gates, Fort Atkinson; Thorpe Merriman, Fort Atkinson; Jess Norenberg, Madison; Clarence Peck, Whitewater; S.N. Schafer, Fort Atkinson; Harvey Sherwood, Gays Mills; Ruth Weigel, LaCrosse; and William J. Willis, Milwaukee. The administrator-chaplain was chosen in October 1960 by a select committee of conference board members. They recommended to the conference board that the Rev. Carroll J. Olm, pastor of St. Paul's Evangelical and Reformed Church, Sheboygan, Wisconsin, be elected to administer the home commencing January 1, 1961. The election took place on October 10, 1960. The Olm family arrived in Whitewater to occupy the parsonage at 244 N. Park Street on December 29, 1960. The Olms accepted the call, having been told that the parsonage had three bedrooms to accommodate their family of five [Carroll and his wife, Marilyn, and their three children, Mark, Elizabeth and James.] It was a surprise and a psychological shock for the Olms to enter the house and find only two bedrooms.

Initially, administration was awkward, with the Fairhaven Board of Directors being asked to mark time until the home's construction was completed. However, everyone was working in covenant toward the goal of developing a ministry for God's older children.

The First Board of Directors—1962. L-R front row: Stanley N. Schafer, Carroll J. Olm, Ruth Weigel, O.J. Gates. L-R back row: Harvey H. Sherwood, Harold Brandenburg, William J. Willis, Thorpe Merriman, Jess H. Norenberg, Clarence N. Peck.

In those very early months, the Fairhaven board was addressing matters pertaining to future operations. The very first concern was legalities! The Articles of Incorporation and Bylaws were already filed. The 501 [c] [3] tax exemption application needed to be addressed. Immediately the expertise of several attorneys surfaced: William Bradford Smith, Madison, who worked predominantly in Madison with Conference Superintendent Jess Norenberg, and two Fairhaven board members, William J. Willis of Foley and Lardner, Milwaukee, who served as the Fairhaven Corporation legal counsel, and Thorpe Merriman, Fort Atkinson.

WILLIAM J. WILLIS

It was William J. Willis to whom board members turned for legal opinions over the years. Willis was a full partner in the Foley and Lardner firm of Milwaukee, Madison, Washington, D.C., and elsewhere. He had the resources of that large firm at his disposal and he could discuss issues with the very best legal minds in the country. Attorney Willis was "tapped" by Jess Norenberg to serve on the Fairhaven Board of Directors though he had not previously been involved in conference activities. Bill knew Jess since high school days, having first met him when Jess directed the senior high church camp, then held at Northland College. At that time Jess was pastor of First Congregational Church, Eau Claire. Later their paths crossed again when they both served on the Student Work Committee at the University of Wisconsin - Madison.

The Fairhaven ministry was saved thousands of dollars annually because Bill did his work gratis [as did the other attorneys.] Everyone had great admiration for William J. Willis. He was repeatedly elected to the board and was annually elected corporate attorney. William J. Willis held the longest continuing board membership in the history of Fairhaven.

William J. Willis—1973

His consecutive years [1961-1991] of involvement totaled 30. On June 23, 1973, he received the Honor Award for Meritorious Service of the Council for Health and Human Service Ministries of the United Church of Christ. In 1987 at New Orleans, Louisiana, the Council for Health and Human Service Ministries of the United Church of Christ named Bill the National Trustee of the Year. Fairhaven Corporation could not have had better legal representation. Bill was articulate, always prompt, intelligent and consistently reflected his Christian faith in his approaches to issues. His professional expertise, his organizational ability, his high standard of ethics, his thorough knowledge of the Fairhaven ministry and his Christian perspectives all contributed to stellar performance by an outstanding servant of God. Bill and his wife, Doris, were faithful members of Plymouth Congregational Church [now United Church of Christ,] Milwaukee.

THE FIRST MEETING OF THE BOARD

The first meeting of the Fairhaven Board of Directors was held on February 11, 1961, in Whitewater, Wisconsin, at the Congregational Church [now United Church of Christ.] The meeting was preceded by a luncheon at the parsonage residence of the Rev. and Mrs. Carroll J. Olm and their children at 244 N. Park Street, Whitewater. Marilyn Olm and Louise Hobbs, wife of Congregational Church pastor Donald S. Hobbs, served the meal.

All members of the board were present and Ruth Weigel served as secretary pro-tem. After the call to order and the opening prayer, Mr. Olm summarized the Fairhaven concept. The physical plans were described using diagrams and drawings, together with a scale of charges for the different living units. The administrator-chaplain also reported that his activities included: contacting resident prospects for the home, selling founders fees, correspondence, conferences with the architect and contractor, conferences with Conference Superintendent Jess Norenberg, reporting to the Wisconsin Congregational Conference Board of Directors and giving attention to publicity.

Board member Harold Brandenburg introduced K. G. Marsden and Gerhard Spielman of the B. C. Ziegler Company to assist in the processing of an FHA loan for the construction of Fairhaven. The means of financing was to be by bond issue secured by a trust indenture, instead of a mortgage secured by a mortgage note.

Superintendent Jess Norenberg reported that it was the opinion of the conference board that it should continue with the financial and legal handling of the Fairhaven affairs until the dedication of the buildings, at which time the Fairhaven board would assume these duties. This was accepted by the Fairhaven board.

At this very early stage of development the board adopted a policy regarding memorials and special gifts to Fairhaven. Such gifts were to be welcomed, memorials or otherwise, at the discretion of the administrator-chaplain. These gifts were to be recorded in a Book of Memories. No labels or plaques were to be displayed, except for major items.

Bylaws of Fairhaven Corporation, previously distributed to the board members by mail, were formally approved.

Director O.J. Gates reported for the Nominating Committee, presenting the following slate of officers: President - Thorpe Merriman; Vice-president and Secretary - S. N. Schafer; Treasurer - Clarence Peck. The officers were elected by unanimous ballot.

A board adopted policy established that admission to the home would be open to persons of any faith as long as they met other admissions requirements.

It was a good first meeting. Genuine enthusiasm was generated, and members were excited about the conference's development of this adventure in living for seniors. The project was the largest initial effort in the history of the conference and the implications of that were scary, but no one "backed-off." There was unanimous endorsement and complete dedication to the cause. It was fully realized that the work was just beginning and that virtually hundreds of things had to be successfully addressed if the project were to succeed.

The second meeting of the board of directors was held on May 15, 1961. A luncheon at the home of Administrator-chaplain and Marilyn Olm preceded the meeting that was held in the parlor of Congregational Church, Whitewater. Board members Brandenburg, Gates, Merriman, Norenberg, Peck Schafer, Sherwood and Olm [ex officio] were present.

Articles of Incorporation and Bylaws were amended to accommodate the FHA loan application.

First National Bank of Fort Atkinson and First Citizens State Bank of Whitewater were approved as depositories for Fairhaven funds.

Director Sherwood reported that the Wisconsin Congregational Conference had adopted a resolution to borrow up to $300,000 at 6% to obtain equity financing for Fairhaven and to guarantee any possible deficits of Fairhaven Corporation. [Note: This resolution was never implemented.]

President Merriman reported that he and Administrator-chaplain Olm had met with Architect Waterman to discuss the increased bids on Fairhaven. The architect's revised fee, based on final construction costs, was accepted.

Administrator-chaplain Olm reported that there were now ten firm resident agreements signed and an additional one nearly completed.

President Merriman projected the creation of a state-wide fund raising committee. Time and again President Merriman persisted with this suggestion. Fund raising was the responsibility of the conference and the conference leadership. This leadership [Jess Norenberg and Richard Wichlei] organized and implemented fund raising efforts and co-opted local leadership whenever and wherever possible. It was surmised that conference leadership resisted the idea of paying fees for professional fund raisers.

On the other hand, a Conference Fund Drive Committee was appointed, composed of the following:

>Robert S. Alward, Fort Atkinson
>Harold G. Andersen, Whitewater
>William F. Edge, Milwaukee
>Marshall Moeser, Port Washington
>Robert L. Smith, Milwaukee
>Max Stieg, Appleton
>Maurice Terry, Milwaukee.

It is documented that the Fund Drive Committee met once. However, it is fair to say that the fund raising rested mainly in the work of Jess Norenberg, who tried to meet emergency fund acquisition by cutting over committee involvement. However, without a doubt, the committee members did their part as individuals, contributing in sundry ways to the cause.

The executive committee composed of President Thorpe Merriman, Vice-president/Secretary Stanley Schafer, Treasurer Clarence Peck, and Administrator-chaplain Carroll Olm, ex officio, held many executive meetings between February 1961 and May 1961:

> February 23, 1961 - Issues: FHA application, architectural plans status and insurance program.
>
> March 8, 1961 - President Merriman, Vice-president/Secretary Schafer and Building Committee chairperson Ned Sperry met without Treasurer Peck and Administrator-chaplain Olm, who could not attend because of the big snow storm. Insurance coverage was discussed.
>
> April 7, 1961 - Architect Arthur Waterman and Building Committee chairperson Ned Sperry were visitors. FHA application and building plans were reviewed.
>
> April 11,1961 - FHA application and engaging of R.H. Batterman, Beloit, Wisconsin, to do a property survey.
>
> April 21, 1961 - Visit to the Milwaukee office of FHA to discuss financial requirements. B.C. Ziegler Company, West Bend, Wisconsin, was represented by Mr. K. G. Marsden.
>
> April 25, 1961 - Met in Milwaukee with the FHA State Director and FHA Regional Attorney Gordon from Chicago. At this meeting William J. Willis agreed to be the attorney of record for Fairhaven Corporation.
>
> May 1, 1961 - Meeting regarding advanced payment of founders fees.

Executive committee members Merriman, Schafer and Peck were beginning to live with the Fairhaven issues every day. It was a lot to ask from these men who had full time responsible professional jobs, especially since the Fairhaven board had no authority to act and since the conference retained complete jurisdiction.

The next significant meeting of the board of directors was held on May 7, 1962, at First Congregational Church, Janesville. It was a joint meeting with the executive committee of the Wisconsin Congregational

Conference Board of Directors in conjunction with the annual meeting of the conference.

Officers were elected as nominated by Director Brandenburg: President - Thorpe Merriman; Vice-president - S.N. Schafer; Secretary-Treasurer - Clarence Peck.

Director Attorney Willis introduced four resolutions:

1] Withdrawal of the FHA application. [See Chapter IV - The Financing.]
2] Approval of a $1,100,000 loan from Anchor Savings and Loan Association, Madison.
3] Amendments to the Articles of Incorporation.
4] Amendments to the By-laws.

Director Willis also reported on the status of the 501 [c] [3] tax exemption application. Fairhaven's exemption from paying Wisconsin Sales Tax was obtained.

Administrator-chaplain Olm reported that construction commenced January 8, 1962. The first units were projected to be ready for occupancy in October or November 1962.

First Citizens State Bank, Whitewater, was approved to be the official depository for Fairhaven Corporation, replacing First National Bank of Fort Atkinson.

CONTINUING CARE CONCEPT ADDED

Three very important and far reaching continuing care policies were introduced by the administrator-chaplain and immediately and unanimously adopted by the board in three separate resolutions.

The first resolution defined temporary infirmary care, which was guaranteed in the early resident agreements. Temporary infirmary care was interpreted to be two weeks of infirmary care without additional charge.

More significant to the entire program was the resolution that the corporation would offer its residents a continuing care program, making necessary rate increases proportionate to the care required. A small six bed infirmary had been incorporated into the original construction drawings. These beds were located in three rooms on the south end of the Central Building's second floor [Building C]. A miniature nursing station and an examination room were also included. Originally, it was envisioned that residents would use these beds when having minor ailments, like the flu. The administrator-chaplain felt the concept was inadequate and unrealistic. He also stated that insufficient staffing was projected, that space would soon be overflowing, and that it would be impossible to operate with any sense of fiscal responsibility. The continuing care resolution embraced changing the construction plans to designate the entire southern half of the Central Building's second floor as the infirmary. Architectural change orders were drafted and a 21 bed infirmary was ensured.

Several things happened immediately: [1] 21 beds provided assurance that every resident would get care when it was needed [short of hospitalization] without having to leave the facility. This was a major step in Fairhaven's philosophy of care and immediately made it easier to attract potential residents and sell founders fees. [2] With 21 beds, the floor could and would be adequately staffed around the clock. The operation would be fiscally sound if not too many beds would be empty. The third resolution was adopted to address that possibility. [3] The administrator-chaplain was authorized, in conjunction with the executive committee, to utilize unused beds for per diem patients [not life lease residents] who needed skilled nursing care and that per diem rates be established to cover the cost of that care.

This was a "breakthrough." Joyfully, the administrator-chaplain went from the board meeting to the pulpit at First Church, Janesville, to address the Wisconsin Congregational Conference in annual session and share the good news. [Note: The text of this address is attached as an addendum to this chapter.]

Enthusiasm for Fairhaven was generated by the corporation directors and by the annual meeting delegates. The continuing care concept was universally accepted. Congregationalists felt good about what their home was going to be. President Merriman presided at the annual meeting of the board of directors on May 23, 1962. Board members Brandenburg, Gates, Merriman, Peck and Schafer ratified and confirmed the actions taken at the special meeting held May 8, 1962, at Janesville.

Through all of 1961 and on into 1962 the Fairhaven Board of Directors and Administrator-chaplain Olm were in covenant with the conference board of directors and conference leadership. They possessed and exercised no power or authority because the conference continued to maintain it would not relinquish responsibility and authority over the books, the construction, the financing and the fund raising. However, by the middle of 1962, all financial records were transferred to the administrator-chaplain with the charge to henceforth be responsible for all Fairhaven's financial involvements. This was a major shift and one that the Fairhaven Board of Directors and administrator-chaplain readily understood. First, the sheer workload to keep the books, make construction payments, etc. was significant. On the other hand, Fairhaven administration consisted of only one person, the administrator-chaplain, who had a full workload already. Second, it made sense to have these important financial transactions made close to the site where on-site observation was essential. Third, the merger of the Wisconsin Congregational Conference churches and the North and South Wisconsin synods of the Evangelical and Reformed Church in Wisconsin was poised for consummation in the fall of 1962. [Actual date: October 26, 1962.] The new United Church of Christ Conference Board of Directors and leadership would have been "hard pressed" to assume the Wisconsin Congregational Conference board's Fairhaven obligations.

Hence, with little forewarning, the books and financing of the project were thrust to the Fairhaven board and administration. The move provided clarification and gave proper authoritative organization to the Fairhaven Board of Directors. The down side was the insecure financing situation. While administration had forewarned the conference about financing shortfall earlier [before construction commenced,] now Fairhaven administration had to work through the problems caused by the shortfall. However, the conference leadership did support administration to its utmost ability and resources throughout those difficult months. [Note: See Chapter V - "The Financing".]

The construction supervision was never officially turned over to the Fairhaven board and administration. It made little difference because the administrator-chaplain, being on the site, had worked closely with the architect and engineers and all the contractors anyway. In all practicality, the Fairhaven board and administration supervised construction.

Fund raising was another matter. Never did the Fairhaven board or administrator-chaplain let fund raising responsibilities be transferred from the conference board and leadership. Fund raising to meet the construction needs alone, was a full time job. Only after construction was completed and the home was operating did Fairhaven, in place of the conference, assume full responsibility for fund raising efforts. First residents arrived November 15, 1962. Construction was declared completed as of June 10, 1963.

It is fitting that initial board members be given tribute in the telling of this story. Directors Merriman, Schafer, Brandenburg and Gates are "lifted up" in the following paragraphs, while other board members [Norenberg, Peck, Sherwood, Weigel and Willis] are highlighted elsewhere.

THORPE MERRIMAN

Fairhaven was fortunate to have Thorpe Merriman as its first president. He gave unstintingly of his time and did not miss executive committee meetings or board meetings. He was dedicated, long-suffering, diligent and always supportive. Thorpe loved his church and he was thoroughly committed to the Fairhaven ministry. He presided effectively; he did legal work; and he was a one man publicity vehicle. Later when residents were present, he visited them and then promoted corporation policies for resident welfare. On June 21, 1984, he was voted the Honor Award for Meritorious Service, a recognition he well could have received many years earlier. In part his citation read: "He was instrumental in the early development of the Fairhaven program and helped to guide it through difficult periods of fund raising, financing, construction and resident recruitment."

Thorpe Merriman—1984

Thorpe voluntarily left the board after serving nine years. Later, when he was elected to directorship again, he was teased as being a "retread." His second membership election came in 1979. Thorpe was a Christian gentleman!

STANLEY SCHAFER

Director Stanley Schafer, a Fort Atkinson banker and member of First Congregational Church, Fort Atkinson, was Fairhaven's first vice-president and secretary. Later, the secretarial duties were linked with the office of treasurer. Stan retained the office of vice-president. Director Schafer knew banking and financing, so he understood the problems faced by Fairhaven in its early development better than most. Stan was involved in the "sticky" financing meetings. After being on the board for two years, he resigned, partly for health reasons. Later he came, with his wife, to reside at Fairhaven. After this wife's death, he continued to enjoy Fairhaven's enhanced living as a widower until his death. Time and again, Director-Resident Schafer made complimentary comments about the Fairhaven ministry.

HAROLD BRANDENBURG

Director Harold Brandenburg knew much about financial affairs. He worked in securities protection at the Wisconsin Department of Securities. Harold, a member of First Congregational Church, Madison, was enamored with the whole Fairhaven thrust. He demonstrated that by showing leadership on the board level and by exerting positive publicity efforts in his local church and community. The name Harold Brandenburg appears time and again in the Fairhaven minutes. He was a man of God, highly respected by others, and always more than ready to do his part.

O. J. GATES

Director O. J. Gates was a practicing Fort Atkinson dentist and a loyal member of First Congregational Church, Fort Atkinson. Director Gates was one of the very early promoters of the conference's thrust in health and human services. He was a mild mannered person who was always ready to go the second mile. With Superintendent Jess Norenberg, O.J. Gates visited retirement homes across the country. He was convinced that the conference's mission was worthy, and he dedicated a good portion of his life to the conference's dream. Director Gates was special at making and/or seconding key motions. Had he not married Resident-to-be Irene Leffingwell, he probably would have been a Fairhaven resident.

These initial directors were a prelude to the long list of quality board members Fairhaven was blessed to receive over the decades. [Succeeding board members' names and contributions will be documented in Volume II.] Fairhaven directors were first class leaders representing a wide variety of Christians from all state geographical regions. There was always a good balance of different backgrounds: clergy/lay members, women/men, business/professional. There was racial inclusion and representation from denominations other than Congregational and/or United Church of Christ. The Fairhaven nominating committee presented the names of board member candidates to the Fairhaven board for approval to recommend the same to the Wisconsin Congregational Conference [later the Wisconsin Conference of the United Church of Christ] nominating committee for election at the conference annual meeting. When the by-laws were changed and the board membership was increased from nine members to 16 members, 12 of the 16 were elected by the conference and four were elected by the board itself.

DIRECTORY: BOARD OF DIRECTORS [1960 - 1990] [Dates below
indicate years of presidency.]

Living

Dr. Robert Ainslie
Mr. Charles C. Block
Mrs. Evelyn J. Boll
Mr. James K. Caldwell
The Rev. Robert L. Cedar
Mr. Alan J. Dunwiddie
Mr. Arnold Evans
Mr. Donald L. Faulkner
Mrs. Fern A. Fellwock
Dr. Eugene R.F. Flug
The Rev. William R. Frank
Dr. E. Paul Gander
Dr. Thomas A. Gobel
Mr. Lyman C. Hauschild
Dr. Fannie E. Hicklin
Mrs. Hildegard Irion
Dr. Kenneth S. Jamron
Mrs. Muril Janisch
Mr. Marshall W. Johnston
    [1980-1990+]
The Rev. Robert L. Johnston
Mr. Russell A. Jones

Deceased

Mr. Leland H. Barker
Mr. Oscar L. Bock
Mr. Harold F. Brandenburg

The Rev. Edward E. Beatty
Mr. Donald D. Doherty
Mr. Russell B. Everhardt

Dr. O.J. Gates
Mrs. Mary Henningsen
Mr. Wayne K. Hinkle
Mrs. Barbara K. Imig [1978-1980]
Mr. E.R. Klassy [1966-1970]
Mrs. Theodora Klug [1973-1974]

Mrs. Mareta Kahlenberg
Mrs. Elizabeth Kincaid
The Rev. Robert J. Kuechmann
Mrs. Jean Lewis
Dr. Thomas S. McLeRoy
The Rev. Robert H. Midgley
Mr. Paul E. Miller
Mrs. H. Jane Morphew
Dr. Louis W. Nowack
The Rev. Max J. Rigert
Mr. John Schneider
The Rev. Dr. Kendrick Strong
Dr. Ralph L. Suechting
Dr. Warren S. Theune
The Rev. Dr. Frederick R. Trost,
    Ex Officio
Attorney John G. Vergeront
Dr. William P. Wendt

Attorney William J. Willis
The Rev. Stanley York
The Rev. Dr. Carroll J. Olm,
    Ex Officio

The Rev. Dr. Clarence F. McCall,
    Ex Officio
Attorney Thorpe I. Merriman
    [1961-1966]
Dr. Carl N. Newpert
The Rev. Jess H. Norenberg
Mr. Clarence N. Peck
    [1970-1973]
The Rev. Trent Rockwell
Mr. Stanley N. Schafer
The Rev. Dr. Egon E. Schieler
The Rev. Harvey H. Sherwood
The Rev. Dr. Robert Stanger,
    Ex Officio

The Rev. Dr. Ralph P. Ley,   Mr. Arthur E. Waterman
    Ex Officio   (1974-1978)
                                             Mrs. Ruth Weigel

Directors considered it an honor to be elected to the Fairhaven board. There were those who never became directors who wished they could have been. One such was Norman Schowalter, West Bend, Wisconsin, an outstanding leader of South Wisconsin Synod of the Evangelical and Reformed Church. He stated that if he had the choice to be elected to any conference board, he would choose the Fairhaven board. That, indeed, contributed stature to the Fairhaven ministry.

ADDENDUM -[Text of the address delivered by Administrator-chaplain Carroll J. Olm at the Wisconsin Congregational Conference annual meeting held at First Congregational Church, Janesville, Wisconsin, on May 8, 1962.]

> A tiny room, a rocking chair,
> Warmth for old bones, clean clothes to wear,
> A reading lamp, a soft white bed,
> A pillow for my weary head,
>
> Sufficient good plain food to eat,
> A little love, some friends to greet,
> A shining faith, a useful task,
> Dear Lord, is that too much to ask?
>
>   Alice Machenzie Swaim

One year ago at Union Church, Green Bay, FAIRHAVEN was presented to you via filmstrip and tape recorder. You saw beautiful colored architect's sketches of the proposed facilities and heard about policies and service. This year you are going to observe the actual progress of construction as we travel to Whitewater tomorrow and tour the FAIRHAVEN grounds. You will be surprised and you should be pleased. God's rich top soil, now piled on little mountains awaits the day when it can be leveled and used to supply life for the roots of green grass, flowers and trees. You will see concrete and steel and wood — pipes, wires and stone — all being made "Christian" because you as a conference have caught a vision to minister to senior citizens of our fellowship and society.

In these days many are asking the questions, "When will the first residents begin to occupy their new homes at FAIRHAVEN?" Mr. George Jakoubek of the T.S. Willis Company, our general contractor, is here to answer that question and to give us a brief report on construction progress: Mr. Jakoubek.

Facilities are important, but not as important as people. FAIRHAVEN is more than buildings — FAIRHAVEN is people — the ones we love and whom we will serve. To date 23 firm applications have been made for residency, involving 30 people. Of these 23 applications, six desire entrance as soon as one building is ready. Nine of the 23 will wait until all construction has been completed and six are on the deferred entrance list. [This means they have made firm application: filling out all required forms, signing the contract, submitting a $500 application fee, but are deferring actual entrance until a later date.] The remaining two of the 23 will not be coming as residents, since both found it necessary to be placed in other homes immediately.

Now it is my honored and extremely happy privilege to introduce to you some of the future residents of FAIRHAVEN. Not all of them were able to be present for a variety of reasons — distance in some cases and illness in others. Miss Schrage, who addressed you last year, is making another speech today at her church in Madison where she is presenting the Story of Fairhaven to four sections of the Women's Fellowship. And then, believe it or not, one of our deferred entrance applicants has just returned from her honeymoon! One of Fairhaven's board members wooed and won the hand of one of our beloved residents. Fortunately, some of the future residents are here and I present them to you at this time.

[Introduce residents] - Dr. and Mrs. E. L. Belknap, Plymouth Church, Milwaukee; Mr. and Mrs. C. H. Walter, First Church, Kenosha; the Rev. and Mrs. Leo L. Duerson, Emmauel Church, Dousman; Mrs. Ruth J. Merrihew, First Church, Oconomowoc; Miss Mary S. Black, First Church, Fort Atkinson; Mrs. Genevieve Spradling, First Church, Sparta.

To the honor of these friends just presented and to the honor of the many other future residents of FAIRHAVEN will you kindly stand so you may received our applause! It is the church's obligation and FAIRHAVEN'S objective to "add life to your years."

Two of the future residents have consented to address the conference. First, a grand fellow, former physics teacher, Lion's Club member, church board and Laymen's Fellowship officer, long time member of First Church, Kenosha — always good for at least one story — Mr. C. H. Walter. Mr. Walter.

Next, a fellow clergyman, who with his wife made the first ministerial application for residency at FAIRHAVEN. They are on the deferred entrance list at present, but we hope it will be real soon when they will find their way through the door of their new apartment at FAIRHAVEN. Pastor of Emmanuel Church, Dousman, the Rev. Leo L. Duerson.

Ignatius Loyola once prayed —

> Lord, teach me to serve thee as thou deservest -
> To give - and not count the cost,
> To fight - and not heed the wounds,
> To toil - and not seek for rest,
> To labor - and not ask any reward except to know
>   that we do thy holy will.

To the end that we might do the will of God: we give - we fight - we toil - we labor! If any one at any time has had any other motive in the FAIRHAVEN enterprise, then he or she has been out of place! FAIRHAVEN is God's — and may it always be God's — that to divine glory and to the praise of God's name this significant ministry be dedicated.

Under God all things are possible and the impossible takes just a little bit longer. Under God you as a conference — not Dr. Jess Norenberg and the conference staff — not Attorney Thorpe Merriman, president, and the FAIRHAVEN board, not the Rev. Carroll J. Olm and the FAIRHAVEN staff — under God you as a conference voted to project this program. It is therefore, your responsibility! When the home succeeds, you succeed — and if the home goes limping along, you share the failure.

You as a conference should be congratulated for your willingness to launch and to continue to support such a tremendous undertaking as FAIRHAVEN. You set your sights high — now as Loyola says - you must give - you must fight - you must toil - you must labor - for no other reason than to know you're doing God's holy will.

FAIRHAVEN must always be an arm of the church! If it is not that — or if there be any intention of not having it continue to be an arm of the church - in its philosophy, in its objective, in its intent, in its support, in its service — then I, personally, do not want to have any more to do with it. . . . .

. . . . .We're anxious to be an arm of the church in the way of residency. There is an important announcement as a result of the FAIRHAVEN board meeting yesterday. It was unanimously decided that continuing care will be offered at FAIRHAVEN with cost adjustments proportionate to the care required. I am certain many of you are happy to hear that.

. . . . .FAIRHAVEN, as an arm of the church, is dependent upon the church for support. Surely, our sights must be lifted! The Evangelical and Reformed people in the state are supporting — over and above their Christian World Mission allotments, over and above World Service, over and above a United Seminary Appeal drive — over and above all these things, they are supporting eight other benevolent projects. In each of the last four years they have raised close to or over $200,000 for these causes. Note, I said in each of the last four years. Raising our sights to match this kind of benevolent activity will help direct FAIRHAVEN to a firm financial future. People, the potential is there — all that is needed is the heart! It is time to think in larger terms — according to your means, of course. For some $10 instead of $1 and for others, thousands instead of hundreds.

Some ask, "Why charge a Founders Fee?" Wouldn't it be thrilling if we wouldn't have to? But how then will the home meet construction payments? Is the conference ready to build the home completely? Some say, "What about charity?" Again, my co-workers and friends, we can only do what you provide for us to do. We are the arm of the church! Show us the way — we'll be glad to do it! But there is no magic wand at Whitewater that erases bills. They must be paid. Our rates are calculated simply to cover operational costs.

We are prepared to serve — we will serve as a not - for - profit home — and we will serve as a charitable home, but you must show the way. FAIRHAVEN is God's and under God all things are possible and the impossible takes just a little bit longer. Under God you have assumed the challenge and the responsibility. And under God it thus becomes an arm of the church.

CHAPTER V

The Financing

"I am the Lord! There is nothing too difficult for me."
Genesis 18:14

The initial financing of Fairhaven fell far short of adequacy! Well meaning conference leadership tried hard to parallel business acumen with faith, but strong desire to get the project going glossed over fiscal hurdles which unless recognized and solved would have bankrupted the proposed project.

FHA

It was the original intention of the conference to finance the project through FHA [Federal Housing Authority.] Jess Norenberg, William Bradford Smith and Harold Brandenburg contributed to the FHA application thrust. The local agency handling the financing would have been the B. C. Ziegler Company of West Bend, Wisconsin. At the first meeting of the Fairhaven board, in February of 1961, Director Brandenburg introduced two Ziegler Company representatives in the persons of K. G. Marsden and Gerhard Spielman. Mr. Marsden reported that the FHA loan was in process with all necessary documents in FHA's hands. It was to have been a 39 year three month loan, with FNMA [Federal National Mortgage Association] taking a portion of it. The means of financing was to be by bond issue secured by a trust indenture, instead of a mortgage secured by a mortgage note. Mr. Marsden explained the advantages of the bond issue and stated that such an issue would be accomplished at no additional cost to Fairhaven. After the Marsden report, Conference Superintendent Norenberg reminded the directors that the conference would continue to handle the financial and legal affairs of Fairhaven until the dedication of the building, at which time the Fairhaven board would assume these duties.

The Fairhaven FHA application became mired in Washington, D. C. bureaucracy! There was delay after delay! Although the conference used every political advantage it could through congressional representatives, etc., no progress was made toward getting the application processed. One source reported that Washington was "re-inventing the wheel" with the Kennedy administration turning FHA upside down. Subsequently, it appeared that the Fairhaven project would not materialize for a long time if it would be financed through the FHA. This was not good news because the merger of the Wisconsin Congregational churches and the North and South synods of the Evangelical and Reformed Church was being projected for the fall of 1962. The Wisconsin Congregational Conference wanted the new Fairhaven facility to be in operation by then.

In desperation, the conference investigated other possible financing sources. No financing agencies were willing to consider the project. First, because it was very large and the conference had no previous experience in the field and second, because the projected Fairhaven program had insufficient equity when measured by normal banking standards.

The FHA deadlock and the inability to negotiate alternative financing caused considerable stress. On September 9, 1961, Jess Norenberg wrote the following about the financing woes:

> In my entire ministry nothing has disturbed me more deeply. It is accurate to say that since the first of June there have not been five nights when in sleeplessness I have not struggled with its problems. Having wrestled for about so long, I wind up with casting this burden upon the Lord with some assurance that [God] will carry it, for I cannot see where we are not doing our best.
>
> There is real tragedy in this labor, nevertheless. The delay has cost us more than $100,000. It has completely undercut us in our promotional program, and it has undermined the faith of many in the entire conference operation. It has gotten so that I dread meeting our people for always the question is the same, "How far is Fairhaven?" Tuesday evening I leave for the north and association programs. I would give my proverbial "eye teeth" to evade this ordeal for I'll need to report on failure of a mission.
>
> It is my determination, however, to remain positive, and to sound no uncertain note. We have done all that has been asked of us, and we have done it promptly. Sooner or later others will fulfill their obligations, and then we can go forward.

ANCHOR SAVINGS AND LOAN

Hope was restored when Anchor Savings and Loan Association, Madison, Wisconsin, lent a listening ear. On November 7, 1961, Attorney William Bradford Smith, Madison, made overtures to Anchor Savings and Loan Association President Al Steinhauer, who expressed considerable interest in the possibility of Anchor involvement in the project. The next Friday, Jess Norenberg escorted Anchor Savings and Loan directors to

Whitewater. Thorpe Merriman and Arthur Waterman joined them there. The group investigated the community, visited the projected site and talked about the possibility of Anchor financing the project. Later, Anchor offered to loan $1,000,000 to Fairhaven Corporation on the condition that the Wisconsin Congregational Conference would co-sign the loan. That requirement made the conference liable for repayment of the Anchor loan should Fairhaven ever default.

There was rejoicing by the conference over this loan negotiation achievement. In conference leadership minds, project construction could now commence. The conference authorized the T. S. Willis Company of Janesville to get on the site and begin building. The T. S. Willis workers arrived at the site, but before they made any significant progress, the administrator-chaplain ordered them to cease and desist. Though he had no authority to act in such manner, that bold step was taken because the financing was not as yet fully secured.

There were never any arguments, but there was strong difference of opinion between the conference leadership and the administrator-chaplain over whether this financing was adequate. Ultimately, the administrator-chaplain called for a special joint meeting of the Fairhaven executive committee and the executive committee of the conference board. He presented a detailed report on the projected conference financing package and why the corporation would fail if the financing package was not strengthened. That meeting was held in the Directors' Room at First National Bank, Fort Atkinson, on November 28, 1961. Harvey Sherwood, chairperson of the conference board and a director of Fairhaven, chaired the meeting.

In essence, the administrator-chaplain presented a typed multi-paged report that documented a $600,000 shortfall in the financing, if the Anchor Savings and Loan Association $1,000,000 loan offer would be accepted. He compared the Anchor financing with the FHA authorized financing, showing how the same shortfall would not occur under FHA. He recommended that FHA authorized financing be the method used by Fairhaven, ensuring success for the project though it was a slower, longer route to take. He was so convinced that the Anchor financing method would spell disaster that he stated his resignation would be effective the first of January 1962, unless the conference would acknowledge the problem.

Clarence Peck, president of First Citizens State Bank, Whitewater, and treasurer of the Fairhaven Board of Directors, supported the administrator-chaplain's position. William Bradford Smith, who had made the initial contact with Anchor Savings and Loan, explained in detail the Anchor proposal. Discussion followed.

By the administrator-chaplain's calculations, the financing shortage was approximately $600,000. Comments were focused on how that amount could be generated to "shore up" the insufficient financing, thus preserving the opportunity to use the conventional loan from Anchor Savings and Loan and, in essence, "save" the project. It was surprising and mildly reassuring to hear how many ideas, most of which were eventually used, surfaced.

Director Sherwood formalized consensus in the following motion that was seconded by Conference Director Richard Shropshire, M.D.:

RESOLVED: That the Anchor Savings and Loan Association, who has submitted a proposal to loan Fairhaven One Million Dollars [$1,000,000,] be advised that such mortgage loan is insufficient to safely finance the construction of Fairhaven and permit the meeting of monthly obligations starting in 1963.

RESOLVED: That FHA loan application be kept alive and that the officers of Fairhaven investigate the possibility of obtaining a conventional loan either from Anchor Savings and Loan, or from other private sources, which loan would be in excess of $1,000,000 and in a sufficient amount to properly finance Fairhaven.

RESOLVED: That if a conventional loan is obtainable a campaign be conducted to obtain gifts and loans of a sufficient amount to fill any gap over the amount of the conventional loan.

The motion passed unanimously!

Chairperson Sherwood urged the administrator-chaplain to remain in his position for at least one additional month, to allow the conference time to show good faith in its efforts to stabilize the financing. The response from the administrator-chaplain was affirmative.

Everyone was aware how significant a meeting it was. Jess Norenberg commented, "This has been the darkest day of my life!"

Subsequently, there was a flurry of action, for the implementation of the resolution was no easy task and there were timetable constraints.

First, Fairhaven President Merriman, Vice-president Schafer, and Secretary-treasurer Peck attempted to interest other financial institutions in offering a convention loan to Fairhaven. There were no interested parties.

Second, William Bradford Smith negotiated with Anchor Savings and Loan President Al Steinhauer and was successful in obtaining an addition to the original loan offer in the amount of $100,000. Credit must be given to William Bradford Smith for his persistent efforts to make the Anchor loan proposal workable. He was convinced that it was the best route to take, specially since it avoided red tape and made it possible to eliminate some expenses which FHA financing would have required. Bill jubilantly announced that an Anchor loan of $1,100,000 was available.

Third, Attorney Director William J. Willis began the process to re-activate the FHA loan application.

Fourth, Jess Norenberg and the Rev. Richard Wichlei, assistant conference superintendent, began to make immediate plans for a fund raising campaign in the conference churches.

Fifth, Jess Norenberg, with assistance from President Merriman, negotiated with the architect and building contractors to obtain waivers of payment from them. In essence, it meant deferring some payment to them for up to four years at 6% interest. Jess also contacted long-standing, loyal Congregationalist Henry Baldwin, industrialist from Wisconsin Rapids, Wisconsin, about the financing shortage. Mr. Baldwin offered a non-interest bearing ten year loan to Fairhaven in the amount of $25,000.

Coverage for the $600,000 shortfall could now be envisioned. By combining all sources of additional financing to the original loan of $1,000,000 offered by Anchor Savings and Loan, completion of construction seemed possible. In summary it appeared like this:

Needed $600,000 additional financing:	$100,000	Anchor Savings and Loan.
	100,000	Payment waiver from T. S. Willis.
	50,000	Payment waiver from Hyland/Hall.
	25,000	Payment waiver from architect.
	25,000	Henry Baldwin loan.
	$300,000	
	300,000	From fund drive.
	$600,000	

The administrator-chaplain announced that he would not resign.

An important joint meeting of the executive committees of the Wisconsin Congregational Conference Board of Directors and Fairhaven Corporation Board of Directors was held at First Congregational Church, Fort Atkinson, on Wednesday, May 23, 1962. The Rev. Kendrick Strong, pastor of First Congregational Church, Janesville, chaired the meeting and offered the opening prayer. Present were: Robert Alward, Fort Atkinson, Harold Brandenburg, Madison, O.J. Gates, Fort Atkinson, Robert Kingdon, Wisconsin Rapids, Thorpe Merriman, Fort Atkinson, Clarence Peck, Whitewater, Kendrick Strong, Janesville, and Richard

Shropshire, Madison, with Jess Norenberg and Richard Wichlei, ex officio.

Fairhaven President Merriman requested a determination of responsibility for Fairhaven. It was agreed that primary responsibility for funding rested with the conference board and secondary responsibility with the Fairhaven board. It was also agreed that use of an outside fund raiser be avoided, if possible.

Third, it was moved by Conference Director Richard Shropshire, M.D., and seconded by Fairhaven Director Harold Brandenburg that "the Board of Directors of the Wisconsin Congregational Conference authorize and endorse a major fund drive by the Wisconsin Congregational Conference for the purpose of raising $300,000 for the FAIRHAVEN home. This fund drive will be the responsibility of the Wisconsin Congregational Conference. The FAIRHAVEN Board of Directors will have secondary responsibility to cooperate and implement the fund drive. The fund drive will be directed by Jess Norenberg, assisted by Richard Wichlei. It will run from June 1, 1962 to June 1, 1963."

The administrator-chaplain made it explicitly clear that unless the fund drive would be immediately successful, the project would be in financial trouble and completion of construction would be jeopardized. It was difficult to make these statements to people who were loved and who had the strongest of faith that success was eminent. However, sensible business acumen dictated that there were difficult days ahead for Fairhaven. Within a few months it came true.

On January 2, 1962, just before construction started, the administrator-chaplain wrote: "I've heard nothing about the culmination of the financing program and the start of construction. I feel like I'm sitting on a barrel of TNT that's going to explode, only I don't know when. Boy, are we anxious around here. Newspaper men call me for publicity jump on others. I've told everyone — 'Not until it's on the dotted line and the machinery comes on the site.' Actually, the article is already written and the envelopes ready for mailing."

THE BIND

Construction commenced January 8, 1962. Certificates of payment for construction were met each month after approval from the architect. Anchor Savings and Loan was the primary source of funds for these payments. Things went smoothly through the September 1962 payment. It was then that Anchor Savings and Loan announced that it would not put another dollar into the project until the churches proved faithful to their commitment to provide fund raising money. Anchor President Steinhauer did not want to exhaust the $1,100,000 loan and then find out that the conference had insufficient funds to complete construction.

On October 11, 1962, Administrator-chaplain Olm wrote to Jess Norenberg:

> Our problem is the interim financing. The only way is ahead, to be sure, but Anchor is bringing pressure and we cannot afford to have construction stop. I would hate to think what that would do to founders fees sales. It has been hard enough building confidence in the program and trying to break down the idea that FAIRHAVEN is expensive — and then sell the lease on top of that. I do not think the average person — even on the board — realizes what it has taken to get the 30 some firm applications that we have.

When Anchor advised Fairhaven of its decision to temporarily withhold further funding, Administrator-chaplain Olm and Director Treasurer Peck met to strategize. Without doubt, Fairhaven was in a financial bind and additional funding had to be secured. It was decided to call the conference leadership to advise them that the predicted bind had come and that help was needed immediately. The October certificate of payment would arrive soon and the contractors had to be paid.

The certificate did arrive. Fairhaven had ten days to make payment of $182,278. Fairhaven had no money in the bank. Anchor Savings and Loan was withholding its money. What a dilemma! Finally, Treasurer Peck suggested we challenge Anchor to provide half the money if the conference would supply the other half. Anchor agreed! The conference was notified that it now had ten days to forward $91,139, one-half of the payment.

The duo team of Norenberg and Wichlei contacted congregations with a fury. By reaching those furthest along on their local campaigns, these men were able to raise the $91,139. Anchor followed with its one-half and the payment was made on time.

It was a big relief! However, the November certificate of payment was soon to come. It arrived in the amount of $149,449. Again heart palpitation! Again dilemma! Again, Fairhaven had no money in the bank and again, Anchor withheld its money! Again a meeting of the administrator-chaplain and the treasurer! Again Anchor Savings and Loan and the conference were challenged to each go half way in meeting the payment! Both agreed!

Certainly, there was pressure on conference leaders to obtain this kind of money [$74,724.50] in ten days.

In fairness to the Congregational conference congregations of the state, let it be said that the church members had pledged to the cause. Most of the pledges were to be paid over a three year period. Fairhaven needed cash on the "barrelhead!" Now, Jess Norenberg and Richard Wichlei developed a new tack. They challenged local congregations to obtain loans from their local banks in the amounts that their members had pledged to the cause, using the pledges as security for the loans. The loans would be paid with the monies that came in as people met their pledges. The idea worked and across the conference many congregations provided needed cash for the project in this way. The November certificate was paid on time.

This was not the end. Construction was scheduled to conclude June 1963. Each month from November 1962 through June 1963 certificates would have to be paid. Fairhaven was in a major financial bind because the financing was inadequate unless the fund drive successfully produced immediate cash. Board members began to realize that the problem was not going to go away. Minutes of a special meeting held at First Congregational Church, Fort Atkinson, at 7:00 p.m., on November 15, 1962, document the broadening of concern in regard to the financial bind. [On that day, November 15, 1962, the administrator-chaplain had driven to Luck [Amery,] Wisconsin, to transport Resident Josephine Finney and her belongings to Fairhaven. It was the first day Fairhaven had residents.]

Those present at the meeting were: Robert Alward, O.J. Gates, E.R. Klassy, [Director S.N. Schafer had resigned from the board and E.R.Klassy, member of First Congregational Church, Fort Atkinson, was elected to complete the Schafer term,] Thorpe Merriman, Clarence Peck, and R. Wickler, with Carroll J. Olm, ex officio. Discussion was held on fund raising activities, the possibility of re-financing, and the possibility of obtaining a second mortgage.

A second emergency meeting of the board of directors was held at Congregational Church, Whitewater, on Sunday, November 25, 1962, at 3:00 p.m. Board members present were: Harold Brandenburg, O.J. Gates, E.R. Klassy, Thorpe Merriman, Clarence Peck, William J. Willis, and Administrator-chaplain Olm [ex officio.]

President Merriman announced that Anchor Savings and Loan had refused to advance further funds from its commitment. He explained plans for arranging re-financing through a Mr. Burnham of Green Bay.

A new Fairhaven Resource Book was distributed and the "Projecting Financing" page was explained by new Director E.R. Klassy. The financing bind was obvious!

After discussion, the following resolution was adopted:

Resolved, that the executive committee shall be delegated full power and authority to negotiate for and execute all papers necessary for securing an additional $300,000 for the Fairhaven building project, through any one or more of the following methods:

1. Authorization shall be broad enough to include an additional loan of $300,000 from Anchor Savings and Loan Association, Madison, Wisconsin, or from others acting together on such loan.

2. Refinancing from any other suitable agencies or corporation in the total sum of $1,400,000.

3. To borrow an additional $300,000 from any person or corporation on a second mortgage on the property of the corporation.

4. The execution of unsecured promissory notes by the corporation to individuals, churches, or corporations who may consent to loan money to the Fairhaven Corporation for such a period of time and at such interest rate of six per cent or less as may be negotiated.

The executive committee is authorized to work out the best terms of paying off the existing mortgage to Anchor Savings and Loan Association in the event that a refinancing loan is obtained.

Two additional resolutions were adopted:

1. A letter of resignation from the Rev. Jess H. Norenberg was read. [Since the Wisconsin Conference of the United Church of Christ became a reality on October 26, 1962, the Norenbergs would be leaving Wisconsin.] It was moved by Director Willis, seconded by Director Klassy that the resignation be accepted effective December 31, 1962. Motion carried.

[Note: In 1963, after resigning from the position of conference superintendent, Jess and Loretta Norenberg moved to New York City where Jess served as Secretary for Pastoral Relations for the Council for Church and Ministry of the United Church of Christ. From 1965 to 1969, Jess accepted interim pastorates at Lake Worth, Florida; Hinsdale, Illinois; Waukesha, Wisconsin; New Smyrna Beach, Florida; Detroit, Michigan; Whitewater, Wisconsin; Rhinelander, Wisconsin; and Edgerton, Wisconsin. Jess and Loretta began residency at Fairhaven on June 23, 1965. Only a little less than four years later on April 22, 1969, Jess died while visiting in the Stevens Point home where he and Loretta had been married in 1926. A dedicated Christian servant/leader was lost to the Church and to Fairhaven. "Well done, good and faithful servant. . . . .!" Matthew 25:21 KJV.]

2. A salary raise was voted for the administrator-chaplain starting January 1, 1963, with a bonus to be paid to him in 1962. [The bonus was paid because directors had discovered that the administrator-chaplain had accepted the call to the Fairhaven ministry at a loss in salary.]

It was anticipated that the December certificate of payment would arrive in the mails in about two weeks. Jess Norenberg, who continued in his conference superintendent capacity through 1962, contacted Mr. T. S. Willis and requested that the T. S. Willis Company try to keep the December certificate of payment as low as possible. Jess used the argument that the company might not need as much money since construction crews would not be working for a week over the Christmas holidays. Mr. Willis, a Christian gentleman who was understanding and considerate, was intrigued by the concept of Fairhaven. He lent a sympathetic ear and did reduce the amount of the December certificate of payment. That was a real credit to the man because certificates of payment are based on what has been paid out in labor costs and/or in purchase of supplies for construction in the previous month.

Pressure was continuing to build. Extreme stress was experienced by those close to the project. During these days, on several occasions, Marilyn Olm was awakened in the middle of the night by the administrator-chaplain who was sitting up in bed screaming. She had to rouse him out of stressful dreaming. Large bunches of the administrator-chaplain's hair fell out during shampooing.

The reduced December certificate of payment arrived in the amount of $100,000. For a third consecutive month, Fairhaven had ten days to make payment. For a third consecutive month, Fairhaven had no money in the bank. For a third consecutive month Anchor Savings and Loan withheld its money. For a third consecutive month, the administrator-chaplain and treasurer met to strategize. For a third consecutive month, Anchor was willing to pay half of the certificate amount if the conference would generate the other one-half. To the credit of Jess Norenberg and Richard Wichlei and the Wisconsin Congregational churches, the $50,000 was obtained from all sources available and the December payment was made. It seemed something short of a miracle that in such a relatively short period of time so much money could be collected from conference accounts and from the congregations through the fund drive. To God be the glory! In less than three months, Congregationalists put $190,863.50 on the Fairhaven "barrelhead." It was a tribute to their loyalty and support and it was a credit to the conference superintendent and his assistant.

By the time the conference leaders had solicited contributions from all the churches, specially "working" all of the potential larger givers, little more money could be "squeezed out of the turnip."

ADDITIONAL OBSTACLES

Additional obstacles were soon to "rear their ugly heads." First, there was no money budgeted for furnishings and equipment. At least $100,000 had to be found somewhere. Second, in the mortgage agreement with Anchor, the conference obligated Fairhaven to making mortgage payments of $7,200 per month commencing January 1, 1963. There was no provision for meeting this obligation. The administrator-chaplain addressed this issue in a December 3, 1962, letter to Jess Norenberg:

> All yesterday morning Thorpe Merriman, Ernie Klassy, Art Waterman and I met with Al Steinhauer and three other Anchor board members for about two and one-half hours at Fairhaven. The Anchor board members received their first good conducted tour throughout the buildings. We answered many of their questions and set out the evaluation that we have made concerning the proposed financing for Fairhaven. They seemed very congenial and it seems our relationship in the future might be on a much better basis with Anchor. I am extremely happy about the meeting. It seems inevitable that one thing will come out of it — the $7,200-a-month payments to Anchor will now be deferred from January 1, 1963, to July 1, 1963. We feel that this is quite a significant step for us and will alleviate our condition tremendously. It certainly was a rather foolish clause to have us pay our indebtedness before the building is even completed.

The six month delay for the commencing of the $7,200 monthly payment was negotiated and eased the bind a mite.

Third, there was no provision made for operating funds [essentially operating deficits].

It was imperative that a second mortgage be negotiated. Authorization had been approved by the Fairhaven Board of Directors at the November 25, 1962, special meeting. It is worthy to note that it was the Fairhaven Corporation Board of Directors that authorized the second mortgage and not the Board of Directors of the Wisconsin

Congregational Conference. No objections were registered from the conference. There should not have been any, for there was no other way. Fairhaven had to be salvaged. The predictions of potential disaster from inadequate financing, documented at the November 28, 1962, special meeting, had become reality.

THE SECOND MORTGAGE

There was no assurance that Anchor Savings and Loan president, Al Steinhauer, would even listen to an appeal for a second mortgage. He had generously increased the original loan from one million to one million one hundred thousand dollars. He had met one-half of the certificate of payment obligations. He had deferred the $7,200 monthly debt retirement payments for six months. On the other hand, he was aware of the gallant effort the churches made to provide funds. Equally important, he did not want the project to fail.

Directors Harold Brandenburg and Clarence Peck and Administrator-chaplain Olm went to negotiate with Mr. Steinhauer at his impressive office in Madison. One could see the Wisconsin capitol building and its dome through the window behind his desk. It was an interesting and historic meeting. Al Steinhauer leaned back on his chair and gave a ten minute tirade on bankers, their inadequacies and their limitations. Next he shifted gears to the ministers and for ten minutes chastised them as lacking business sense. The negotiators did not argue with him.

Eventually, Mr. Steinhauer "wound down." Then the hard realities of the Fairhaven situation were summarized. Positives were also enumerated. [Five residents were already living in their apartments. Over 30 firm applications were committed. There was positive statewide publicity. The Congregationalists had proved that they wanted the project and were willing to support it. The Wisconsin Congregational Conference had co-signed the first mortgage.] The negotiators did not make any pleas. There was no excessive promise making. Perhaps Mr. Steinhauer had made up his mind previously to provide a second mortgage. After the Fairhaven representatives had finished with their presentation, Mr. Steinhauer said, "Anchor Savings and Loan does not want to operate a home for senior citizens in Whitewater. How much money do you need?"

Administrator-chaplain Olm said, "$200,000," and then outlined the financial projections. Then Mr. Steinhauer responded, "We will provide you with that $200,000, but do not come back here for any additional money because you will not get it!" The administrator-chaplain replied, "Our projections are sound. We won't need the entire $200,000." Steinhauer said, "That I do not believe. There will be change orders.

There will be unforeseen expenses. You will use that $200,000, but any additional money you will have to get elsewhere, not from Anchor."

It was a time for rejoicing. Fairhaven would be completed. The representatives drove home with a feeling of relief and a sense of satisfaction.

Official authorization for the second mortgage was given by the Fairhaven Board of Directors on January 16, 1963. Present were: Directors Merriman and Klassy, along with Administrator-chaplain Olm. By waiver vote: Directors Brandenburg, Gates, Peck, Sherwood and Willis.

The financing bind was over. However, strict supervision over construction costs was now imperative. Especially change orders had to be minimized. The architect and contractors were apprised of the situation. Every attempt would be made to prove to A. C. Steinhauer that the entire $200,000 second mortgage would not be needed, that some bankers are effective and that some ministers do have business sense. Henceforth, whenever a change order increasing costs would come through, the administrator-chaplain initiated another change order that would reduce construction costs in like amount. When a $7,500 change order was required, over and above the donation given by Nellie Fowler of Whitewater, to complete the beauty shop for the Central building, it was necessary to find a deletion of $7,500. After a careful scrutiny of the plans, a Lannon stone wall, which was designed to project from the B-C walkway west toward the north-south sidewalk was deleted. The Lannon stone wall projecting from the C-D walkway west toward the north-south sidewalk was **not** deleted. These walls were incorporated into the landscaping plans to partially compensate for the five foot differential that existed between the foundation of Building E and the foundation of Building A. No one ever noticed or commented on the fact that the wall had been deleted. The $7,500 reduction change order was realized, the beauty shop construction costs were covered, and the building budget was again balanced.

At the conclusion of construction, Fairhaven sent a check in the amount of $21,000 to Anchor Savings and Loan. It represented the unused first mortgage monies. Only $130,000 of the $200,000 second mortgage money was used. Mr. Steinhauer was impressed and, henceforth, always qualified his remarks about ministers having no business sense by saying ". . . . . with the exception of Fairhaven's administrator-chaplain."

Two very positive factors assisted tremendously in Fairhaven being able to "work through" its initial financial woes — specially in regard to meeting its early debt repayment schedule and absorbing operational losses until sufficient residency was achieved. Those two positive factors were: [1] the very generous benevolent support from the new Wisconsin Conference of the United Church of Christ; and [2] the contribution made by Fairhaven Director E. R. Klassy toward Fairhaven's financial organization and planning.

The Lord said, "Your heart will always be where your treasure is." [Matthew 6:21.] The Wisconsin Conference United Church of Christ gifts to Fairhaven through the United Conference Appeal had "life-saving" effect for the operational years of 1963 and 1964.

For the year 1963, the conference approved a $60,000 United Conference Appeal budgetary item for Fairhaven operations. Historically, the conference raised between 75% to 80% of its United Conference Appeal budget. In September 1963, Administrator-chaplain Olm wrote: "The conference has continued to make some monthly payments to us on its pledge for underwriting the operational budget. So far, we have received approximately $2,500 a month, instead of the allotted $5,000 per month. We are grateful! Perhaps they will increase our allotment between now and the end of the year. However, the conference has its fiscal problems, too. . . . . ."

For the year 1964, Fairhaven administration requested $40,000 from the United Conference Appeal. The conference leaders had expected Fairhaven to come in with another $60,000 request. It was reported that both surprise and pleasure were expressed. When the United Conference Appeal budget was finalized for the year 1964, a figure of $58,000 appeared for Fairhaven.

For the year 1965, the budgeted allotment dropped to $52,000, after Fairhaven had requested $20,000.

Conference support in the initial years was "seed money" that assisted in the process of nurturing the "acorn" during its growth into an "oak."

The second positive factor was the financial planning contributed by Director E. R. Klassy. In a February 23, 1963, letter to Jess Norenberg, Administrator-chaplain Olm wrote:

> The financial statement and projected construction financing plan is the result of E. R. Klassy's work. He certainly has been a gem in getting our situation clarified. We worked long and hard to get this projection in order and to try to make sense out of the many accounting reports we got from Madison [conference] concerning the early stages of the program. Though the figures did not all jibe, Ernie was able to set up the books and the enclosed report was distributed to the executive committee of the confer-

ence board on February 1, 1963. Another follow up report will go to the full conference board on April 1, 1963.

Using actuarial tables, Director Klassy projected estimated founders fee income for the corporation over the course of the mortgage repayment years. His estimated founders fee income/payment schedule brought a realistic financial projection for the Fairhaven directors. It also was a decisive factor in the negotiation for the second mortgage.

E. R. KLASSY

God gave a special gift to the Fairhaven ministry when, by providence, E. R. Klassy became a member of the board of directors. Director Klassy brought a pleasing personality and a wealth of financial experience to the board. He was the retired president of the James Manufacturing Company, Fort Atkinson, and vice-president of Citizen's State Bank, Fort Atkinson. Furthermore, he had given more than two decades as one of the trustees of Fort Atkinson Memorial Hospital [now Fort Atkinson Memorial Health Services.] Ernie was well organized, translated projection concepts to paper reports and brought fiscal conservative policies for consideration. He was thorough, accurate and persever-

E.R. Klassy—1966
Zahn Studio

ing. In 1966, he was elected president of the board, and on June 27, 1970, he received the Honor Award for Meritorious Service.

CLARENCE PECK

The name of Director Clarence Peck, Whitewater, does not appear often in the early Fairhaven records because he served as secretary of the board during the formulative years. However, Director Peck was a stalwart when the valleys of despair were experienced. Clarence was a member of Congregational Church, Whitewater, a trustee of Fort Atkinson Memorial Hospital, and the president of First Citizens State

Bank, Whitewater. With Clarence, First Citizens State Bank stood solidly behind the Fairhaven concept and program. Director Peck was always available — always accessible. Never did he offer "off the cuff" or "slip-shod" advice. He was a solid conservative who deserves credit for helping to keep the Fairhaven ministry from failure. As treasurer of the board, he projected innumerable ideas, which when implemented, kept Fairhaven solvent. Fairhaven never had a finer, more dedicated, talented and humble friend. He became president of the Fairhaven Board of Directors in 1970. On June 26, 1971, he received the Honor Award for Meritorious Service.

Clarence Peck—1971
Carl Jorgenson

SUMMARY LETTER

The construction financing dilemmas of Fairhaven were summarized in the following letter from the administrator-chaplain to the Wisconsin Conference of the United Church of Christ president and treasurer:

December 31, 1962

The Rev. C. F. McCall
2719 Marshall Court
Madison, Wisconsin

Mr. Norman A. Schowalter
509 South Sixth Avenue
West Bend, Wisconsin

Dear Christian friends:
This letter to you fine gentlemen is long overdue, but pressures of many sundry matters have forced me to delay writing until now. Ever since the October consolidation meeting in Madison it has been my intention to write to you in an attempt to

bring clarification [to the greatest extent possible] for your thinking and future action regarding FAIRHAVEN CORPORA-TION and its relation to the Wisconsin Conference of the United Church of Christ.

Now that January 1, 1963, has almost arrived, FAIRHAVEN — along with all the other benevolent agencies of the United Church of Christ in the State of Wisconsin — is looking to the new conference for guidance and counsel and support. As we all know, the new conference assumes the assets and the liabilities of the two Evangelical and Reformed Synods and the Congregational Conference.

Of all the institutions of the Wisconsin Conference, FAIRHAVEN is in one of the most crucial situations. This is partly true because FAIRHAVEN is brand new, still in construc-tion. This is partly true because FAIRHAVEN is an exceptionally large undertaking — at its inception the largest of either of the traditions in the state. This is partly true because the consolida-tion of the synods and the conference comes right during the time that FAIRHAVEN needs the most support. Most of all it is in a crucial situation because of the manner in which FAIRHAVEN has been financed.

As predicted — FAIRHAVEN is facing a financial bind due to the lack of sufficient capital funds for construction. For the last three months we have faced large certificates of payment with-out knowing from where the monies would come. In each case we have been able to squeak by. Three or four more such crises will be met in the months to follow. Though valleys of despair have been experienced, it is the faith and the conviction of all those involved that the program will be a success and that all obstacles will be met. To accomplish this, a great deal of work will have to be done and many sources will have to come to FAIRHAVEN'S support.

For you gentlemen to fully appreciate the position of the FAIRHAVEN board and the administrator-chaplain in this entire matter, it is necessary for me to advise you that the board was elected to OPERATE the Home and the administrator-chaplain was engaged to OPERATE the Home. It was always understood — and I continue to maintain this in spite of future statements of action in this letter — that the WISCONSIN CONGREGATIONAL CONFERENCE and its EXECUTIVE BOARD, functioning through the conference staff is responsible for the financing and construction of the Home.

Though this is true — and because the financing bears so much on future operations of the Home — back on November 28, 1961, just before contracts were to be signed with Anchor Savings and Loan for a $1,000,000 loan for FAIRHAVEN'S construction, I requested a hearing before the executive board of the conference and the FAIRHAVEN Board of Directors. At this meeting I presented in written report a prediction of the present financial bind and urged the conference to seek other financing. [This report is available at your request.] I offered my resignation as administrator-chaplain and concluded my report with these words: "I am completely and irrevocably convinced that Fairhaven should not be financed under the Anchor Savings Plan . . . . . I recommend that proceedings with Anchor Savings be discontinued immediately and that financing proceed with the B. C. Ziegler Company in spite of possible delays. It is my further recommendation that a major capital funds drive be organized immediately to gain additional funds. . ." Mr. Clarence Peck, president of First Citizens State Bank of Whitewater and secretary-treasurer of FAIRHAVEN, supported me in this meeting.

As a result of the meeting, the conference retraced its steps and negotiated for a $1,100,000 loan [$100,000 additional] from Anchor Savings and Loan. They also obtained $150,000 in waivers from the contractors on a four year at six percent basis. The conference also promised to begin efforts for a major Capital Funds Drive. My evaluation was that if the conference could raise $300,000 in a fund drive by June 1st, 1963, that adequate financing would be available. A published goal of $300,000 was sent with quotas totaling over $400,000 given out. Again the responsibility for the Fund Drive rested with the conference through its executive board and staff. This has been acknowledged in formal resolutions by them. Just in recent days has the drive brought over $100,000. Efforts continue! FAIRHAVEN has 1963 — a period of grace extended by the new conference — to conclude the drive so that all benevolent agencies will be entering the United Conference Appeal program in 1964 on an equal basis.

Mr. Thorpe Merriman, an attorney from Fort Atkinson and former Jefferson County District Attorney and president of FAIRHAVEN [Board of Directors], has been exceedingly concerned about needed coordination and organization in the Fund Drive and has repeatedly appealed for full time fund drive director help. In a recent letter Mr. Merriman states: "The real diffi-

culty the Fairhaven board faces is that it has all of the obligations, most monthly building payments to meet, and no real
'power' to raise money. They had always been with the conference which was somewhat slow in seeing the urgent need to
push such a large project. It took perhaps five months to get the
conference officials to understand that real action was imperative as Fairhaven had nothing except money which was dribbling
in in small quantity to get its share of building costs. This
dichotomy is what so frustrated the Fairhaven board. It took
many lengthy meetings to drive home the point that it takes more
than inspiration by a few and the mere asking to open the floodgates of contributions. It seems to me it takes real organization
and follow-through to accomplish this."

One of the real problems that the FAIRHAVEN board and the
administrator-chaplain now face is that the Wisconsin
Congregational Conference has given way to the United
Conference. The old Wisconsin Congregational Conference
Board of Directors no longer has legal powers and has given way
to the new board of the United Conference.

Lest the FAIRHAVEN financing flounder any more and
assuming that the new United Board would not want to handle
the financing of FAIRHAVEN, the FAIRHAVEN board has taken
steps to now direct the rest of the financing of the project. I am
quite certain that the board is doing so reluctantly in some ways
— but zealously in others.

Immediately after the FAIRHAVEN executive committee
realized that this was undoubtedly inevitable, we set out under
Mr. E. R. Klassy's direction to bring some clearer financial direction to the program. [Mr. Klassy is the former president of James
Company in Fort Atkinson — 12 years — and is vice-president of
FAIRHAVEN.] Though we did not want to take a prerogative that
was not ours, we nevertheless prepared a proposed financing
schedule and presented it to the Anchor Savings and Loan
Association and to the conference board and staff members. I do
not know whether or not the conference board had a real schedule before that time.

After the October consolidation meeting we prepared a more
complete report and presented it to a number of key people who
could help us in our weakest areas. A copy of this report is being
mailed to you. I trust you will read its contents thoroughly and
carefully. Especially the Project Financing Schedule on about the
seventh page. Thus far we have been able to meet this schedule.

It is our hope and intention to continue to meet it, but help will be needed.

At our last executive meeting the committee took action in two directions: 1. Mr. E. R. Klassy is appointed as FINANCING COORDINATOR; 2. Immediate appointment of a Fund Drive Chairman to replace Jess Norenberg and Dick Wichlei to be made by FAIRHAVEN President Thorpe Merriman in consultation with Dick Wichlei.

Since the conference has about $200,000 left to raise on the needed $300,000 we have need of about $200,000 to get us over the hump. Negotiations have been made with Anchor and it is willing to give us a second mortgage of $200,000 at six percent payable in four years. The fly in the ointment is that Anchor demands that the conference co-sign the note. This was also demanded for the first financing loan of $1,000,000. Since the Wisconsin Congregational Conference has given way to the United Conference, the co-signing will have to be by the United Conference, if at all. Proper presentation of this matter will be made at the January meeting of the United Conference board.

We have explored all possibilities and have found that second mortgage money costs 12% interest per year or one percent per month, which indicates that the terms of the second mortgage offered by Anchor Savings and Loan are exceedingly desirable.

I hope this will clarify our present status. The letter is lengthy and I thank you for reading it to the end. Though this might leave a shadow over the FAIRHAVEN program in your minds — may I be quick to share with you the many, many wonderful things about our project. It is already successful with five satisfied residents in Building E. They continue to tell me how happy and comfortable they are. About 10 more residents will be coming between now and February 1st. Thus far we have processed applications involving over $250,000 worth of founders fees to date, which represents about 25% of capacity. Our founders fee schedule as listed in the report should be met as projected.

Everywhere we go people are excited about FAIRHAVEN. Well might they be for our site is unexcelled, the facilities are outstanding, and the residents are the "salt of the earth." The conference is already proud of what it is doing here and there is not a doubt in my mind that the conference will give a most significant, loving, charitable ministry in many decades to come.

Two brief comments in closing: 1] A former chief engineer of new construction for the University of Wisconsin [now the University of Wisconsin - Madison] advised us upon touring the FAIRHAVEN site that in his 53 years experience with buildings that he has never seen a building constructed finer than FAIRHAVEN'S. 2. We are now processing through our first resident who is coming in without needing to pay a founders fee. It will be $5,250 worth of charity. Early in 1963 certain individuals are making it possible for us to bring in another person for $9,000 worth of charity. That should speak well about the intentions of FAIRHAVEN regarding charity work.

Please accept my personal greetings and best wishes in this holiday season. I am looking forward to working closely with you gentlemen in the days to come. Please feel free to ask questions or request information of any kind at any time.

Sincerely yours,

/s/ Carroll J. Olm

ADDENDUM - FUTURE ATTAINMENTS

Once the construction financial bind was overcome, Fairhaven slowly attained stability and strength. The following will briefly summarize the level of success Fairhaven achieved by the end of three decades:

The first indicator of success was the continued leasing of available apartments. Full occupancy was achieved by June 1964.

In June of 1963, the $21,000 balance of first mortgage money was applied on the second mortgage. $70,000 of the $200,000 second mortgage money was never used and was returned to Anchor Savings and Loan Association.

Final payment on the second mortgage was made in October 1963. By May 1964, other secondary financing obligations were liquidated as follows:

$21.000 - Waterman note.

22,500 - Baldwin note.

50,000 - Hyland, Hall & Co. note.

75,000 - of the $100,000 T. S. Willis note.

$7,200 per month payments on the first mortgage commenced July 10, 1963.

On March 1, 1965, a $100,000 prepayment was made on the mortgage and the interest rate dropped by one-quarter percent.

The final payment of the T. S. Willis note, in the amount of $25,000, was paid August 1, 1967.

A $7,000 [no interest] note to First Congregational Church [now United Church of Christ], Appleton, Wisconsin, was paid in January 1968.

A loan of $5,600 from First Congregational Church [now United Church of Christ], Waukesha, Wisconsin, was liquidated.

A major expansion of over $2,000,000 occurred in 1970.

Final payment on the first mortgage [$1,100,000] was made on June 10, 1980.

Additional expansions came in 1983-1984 and 1988-1989.

Three goals of the administrator-chaplain were realized prior to his turning over administrative responsibility to his successor:

1] That Fairhaven's local, statewide, and national image would be one of quality operation, with a satisfied residency and a respected staff.

2] That there would be no indebtedness to outside institutions.

3] That the Deferred Annuity Fund [endowment] would reach the $500,000 level. [$750,000 was attained.]

CHAPTER VI

Publicity and Fund Raising

"The business that considers itself immune to the necessity for advertising sooner or later finds itself immune to business." *1
Derby Brown

"Make all you can, save all you can, give all you can!" *1
J. Wesley

The success of Fairhaven's ministry was [and will continue to be] directly proportionate to the degree Fairhaven related to the churches of the Wisconsin Conference [Congregational formerly and United Church of Christ since 1962], the State of Wisconsin, local governmental bodies, prospective residents and potential donors.

Creating a positive image for Fairhaven was initially a gigantic task for several reasons:

[1] Little money was budgeted for public relations purposes. The 1961 promotional costs of $342 increased to $1,367 in 1962. No public relations person was engaged. No professional fund raiser was ever used by the conference or for Fairhaven directly.

[2] The concept of this ministry was innovative to the State of Wisconsin. People had not heard of this type programming and had to be educated about it. [See Chapter "The Concept."]

[3] Initially, people had a difficult time understanding how upfront capital payment fee worked and why it could be viewed positively.

[4] Fairhaven was the Wisconsin Congregational Conference's *first* attempt at health and human services for the aging.

It was imperative that information be disseminated by whatever means of conveyance available, without exacting much expenditure. Several methods were pursued to address this goal.

*1 Reprinted from Useful Quotations published 1934.

CHURCH LIFE

For years the conference published *Church Life* once a month and distributed it to the congregations of the Wisconsin Congregational Conference. The cost of printing and sending this magazine was carried in the conference budget. This vehicle was printed on glossy paper, utilized multi-colors and made extensive use of photographs. Fairhaven made liberal use of *Church Life*. Each month the administrator-chaplain would prepare feature articles on the progress of the Fairhaven thrust, on resident recruitment and on fund raising, particularly appealing for local congregational members to include Fairhaven in their wills. These efforts proved to be effective. Members were kept abreast of progress. Many persons requested information for future residency and a significant number made residency application. The requests to remember Fairhaven in wills paid great dividends. For decades, Fairhaven received small and large legacies, partly as a result of that effort.

SERMONS, LECTURES, TALKS AND PROGRAMS

The administrator-chaplain brought the Fairhaven mission message to the people of the conference through Sunday morning sermons. During the first three years he preached on Sundays to nearly every congregation of the conference. Week day [usually evening] programs were also provided frequently. After long hours of administration each day, the added responsibility to preach on Sundays and/or to spend evenings giving talks or showing pictures, resulted in considerable fatigue.

For example: First Congregational Church, Wisconsin Rapids, invited the administrator-chaplain for a Sunday of Fairhaven mission sharing. It resulted in the following schedule:

4:00 a.m. - Arise and prepare for leaving.

5:00 - 8:00 a.m. - Drive 150 miles to Wisconsin Rapids.

8:15 - 9:00 a.m. - Preach at the early service.

9:15 - 10:15 a.m. - Speak to the Sunday School.

10:30 - 11:30 a.m. - Preach at the second service.

11:30 -12:15 p.m. - Speak and field questions at the congregational meeting. [$15,000 was voted for the Fairhaven project.]

12:30 - 1:45 p.m. - Luncheon and discussions with influential members at the Mead Inn.

2:00 - 3:15 p.m. - Visited a prospective Fairhaven resident in her home. [Application was made that afternoon. The applicant later resided at Fairhaven.]

3:20 - 4:00 p.m. - Visited Leland and Helen Bass Barker at their home.

[Leland Barker later became a member of the Fairhaven Board of Directors. Leland and Helen Bass Barker and their son, Hartley Barker, and his wife, Ruth Baldwin Barker, were some of the most staunch supporters of the Fairhaven ministry, donating much to enhance the physical surroundings. They also orally shared their enthusiasm about the ministry to others.]

4:00 - 7:00 p.m. - Drove 150 miles home from Wisconsin Rapids.

It was not always easy to blend the Fairhaven message into the various spiritual emphases of the church year. For example: After being on the job for three months, the administrator-chaplain was invited to preach a sermon on the Fairhaven ministry for the third Wednesday night Lenten service at a church in Beloit, Wisconsin. This presented a dilemma, since traditionally Lent focuses on the passion, suffering and crucifixion of Jesus Christ. Question: How does one, during Lent, rationalize preaching about the church's responsibility to God's older children, instead of focusing on the message of the cross? He thought about it and he prayed about it. Surely God would provide a sense of direction. A week before the service the answer came from John 19:25-27:

Jesus' mother stood beside his cross with her sister and Mary the wife of Clopas. Mary Magdalene was standing there too. When Jesus saw his mother and his favorite disciple with her, he said to his mother, "This man is now your son." Then he said to the disciple, "She is now your mother." From then on, that disciple took her into his own home.

If Jesus on the cross, in the very act of atonement, remembered to care for his mother, is it not appropriate, in the season of Lent, to focus on the care of our elderly?

Educational institutions extended invitations for the administrator-chaplain to give class lectures or school talks. He lectured at University of Wisconsin - Whitewate;, University of Wisconsin - Oshkosh; Lakeland College, Sheboygan; United Theological Seminary, New Brighton, Minnesota; Waukesha Technical College, Waukesha; and at the Volunteer Training Center of the United Church of Christ, Pottstown, Pennsylvania.

Church and state organizations, community service clubs, schools, associations, state and national conventions — all invited the administrator-chaplain to address their groups on aging, techniques of service,

Fairhaven itself, rules and regulations for those caring for the aging, methods of financing facilities to provide for the aging, etc. Sometimes he made use of colored slides or other visual aids. Hundreds of such presentations were made, mostly in the State of Wisconsin. In the first year on the job, the administrator-chaplain drove 38,000 miles in behalf of Fairhaven. Over the course of 29 years, the administrator-chaplain gave church and association convention keynote addresses in more than half of the states in the union.

The Rev. William Edge, Milwaukee, created and produced an excellent eight mm colored motion picture for Fairhaven promotion. Announced residents-to-be [and later Fairhaven residents] helped to promote by being available for program presentation. They were specially effective in local congregations when they shared the reasons they chose to live at Fairhaven. On April 28, 1970, the Rev. Gale Wolf, executive director of Winnebago Children's Home [now Sunburst, Inc.] wrote, "As I told you many times before, the best PR you have are those many happy occupants who eagerly await an opportunity to tell of the joys of living at Fairhaven. . . . . 'Where life is added to years.'"

Thus sermons, lectures, talks and programs became the means by which considerable publicity was generated for the project. Fortunately, it didn't cost any dollars to do it.

THE PROGRESS REPORT

A mailing list was developed gradually, composed of those persons who showed any interest in what Fairhaven was trying to do. While some were potential persons for residency recruitment, others were younger and simply wanted to be kept abreast of what was happening — hence, the name Progress Report. In other words, here was a vehicle to provide information on how the Fairhaven ministry was progressing: physically, educationally, numerically, programmatically, financially, fund raising wise, etc. The Progress Report was designed to be read immediately upon arrival in the mail. It was initially sent out monthly, later quarterly. Since budget was a concern, administration decided to mimeograph it "in house" on gold colored paper [representative of the golden years.] Keeping it short, usually one page [on both sides] was important. The mimeographed copy made it more intimate, warm, homey.

The progress reports were gratefully received by readers and the format was not changed until the 1990's.

NEWS RELEASES, FEATURE STORIES
AND RADIO/TV INTERVIEWS

Any item considered sufficiently newsworthy to capture the interest of newspaper readers was sent out to daily and weekly newspapers in the state. These articles, written by the administrator-chaplain, were mimeographed on gold colored paper which had printed FAIRHAVEN NEWS RELEASE letterhead. Each year dozens of releases were distributed to radio and TV stations, in addition to newspapers. Often newspaper photographers came for pictures to support the articles. Most releases were printed by the Whitewater Register, Janesville Gazette and the Jefferson County Daily Union Leader and often broadcast by the Fort Atkinson, Janesville, and Whitewater radio stations. Occasionally, the major state newspapers printed a Fairhaven article. i.e. - "Miss America Visits Fairhaven" or "Governor Applauds Fairhaven."

Feature stories were distributed and usually used. Occasionally the Milwaukee Journal, the Milwaukee Sentinel and the Wisconsin State Journal [Madison] feature writers highlighted some aspect of a Fairhaven resident or the Fairhaven ministry. Three lengthy, complimentary articles on the ministry appeared in the "Jaunts With Jamie" column of the Milwaukee Sentinel. The instigator of these articles was Resident Esther Dunham, a former Milwaukeean, who for 20 years was a registered nurse at Milwaukee Children's Hospital. Once a lengthy feature story on Fairhaven appeared in a major state newspaper and the administrator-chaplain was quoted directly, while in fact, no one had made a contact with him. [Fortunately, the quotation could easily have been said by the administrator-chaplain.]

National exposure was also helpful. *Money Magazine* did a feature story. In the March 1964 issue of *Senior Citizen*, published by Senior Citizens of America, Washington, D.C., Fairhaven was featured with three other homes from Missouri, Tennessee and Washington, D.C., in an article "Apartments as Retirement Homes." In 1972, the national publication *A.D.* of the United Church of Christ chose to feature Fairhaven in an eight page article, with pictures, to focus on the denomination's work in health and human service ministries. A U.S. Government Division on Aging representative from Georgia flew to Whitewater specifically to visit Fairhaven. After surveying other facilities, she chose Fairhaven as one of five outstanding homes in America. Several Wisconsin government and state association magazines and reports featured Fairhaven. Hundreds of articles and photographs from newspapers and magazines filled many historical albums.

The administrator-chaplain appeared for interviews on Milwaukee television stations WISN-TV and WITI-TV and on Madison's Channel 27.

Invitations also were accepted for radio interviews at Fort Atkinson, Janesville, Watertown and Whitewater.

How do you put a value on the free of charge publicity Fairhaven received through the newspapers, magazines, various reports and radio/TV? It was the kind of exposure that cannot be bought.

CONFERENCE AND ASSOCIATION MEETINGS

During Fairhaven's formulative years, the Wisconsin Congregational Conference, which gave Fairhaven birth, always found time on conference annual meeting agendas and on the various association meeting agendas to publicize Fairhaven. This PR was accomplished formally by addresses, question and answer sessions, audio-visuals, mission fairs, etc. The impact generated positive results. Not only conference leaders and conference pastors, but also dedicated lay members, made significant contributions for the promotion of Fairhaven.

RUTH WEIGEL

In the LaCrosse Association and on the conference level, Ruth Weigel, member of First Congregational Church, LaCrosse, was a dynamic force. She kept the project in the forefront of the Congregational mission thrusts. Ruth was in key positions to promote the cause. [i.e. - Association and conference boards, Congregational Women's board.] This talented, personable, dedicated Christian, along with her husband, Carrol, gave endless hours for the conference and Fairhaven. She became a member of the initial Fairhaven Board of Directors and on November 11, 1978, she received the Honor Award for Meritorious Service.

Ruth Weigel—1989

In 1962, a Fairhaven Resource Book was printed. Two thousand two hundred fifty copies were distributed to pastors of the conference and to selected lay people who were in key positions.

Crawford Thayer, First Congregational Church, Fort Atkinson, was a talkative, talented, energetic contributor to the promotion of Fairhaven. He effectively solicited the men of the churches to support the cause. He used the Wisconsin Congregational Laymen organization as his platform. Along with Thorpe Merriman, Fort Atkinson, he founded the Century Club [100 Congregational men each contributing $100 to the Fairhaven project.]

SPECIAL EVENTS

Groundbreaking on October 2, 1960, was the first special event. Its good attendance, along with the energetic enthusiasm created for the project, set the standard for the celebration of future milestones. An estimated 500 to 600 people attended the Groundbreaking; some at the ceremonies held at the Congregational Church [now United Church of Christ], some at the site where the first spades of ground were symbolically lifted, and some at both places. The conference had publicized the Groundbreaking event through its printed vehicles to all local congregations. Other denomination affiliated people in the area were welcomed

Groundbreaking—October 2, 1960. L-R: Carroll J. Olm, Robert Midgley, Jess H. Norenberg, Donald S. Hobbs.

via announcements in their church bulletins and/or by reading the news-papers.

Principals officiating at the Groundbreaking were:

Donald S. Hobbs, pastor, Congregational Church, Whitewater.
Robert Midgley, pastor, Lake Edge Congregational Church, Madison, and moderator of the conference.
Jess H. Norenberg, conference superintendent.
Carroll J. Olm, administrator-chaplain elect.
Charles Trinkle, Whitewater City Manager.
Arthur E. Waterman, architect, Fort Atkinson.
Richard Wichlei, assistant conference superintendent, Madison.

CORNERSTONE LAYING

It was estimated that 1,800 people attended the Cornerstone Laying ceremonies, held on October 14, 1962. 1,500 programs were passed out [exhausting supply] by 3:00 p.m. By this time Buildings D and E were structurally progressing, with some apartments ready for open house. The first floor of Building C was "roughed in", with concrete slabs and the four story high building beams were in place, standing like sentinels against the sky. A portion of the front canopy was completed. The cornerstone was located at the south side of the front entrance of Building C.

The crowd gathered at the partially built front entrance with the following people participating in formal ceremony:

Robert Kingdon, pastor, First Congregational Church, Wisconsin Rapids and moderator of the conference.
Kendrick Strong, pastor, First Congregational Church, Janesville, and conference board chairperson.
Jess H. Norenberg, conference superintendent.
Richard Wichlei, assistant conference superintendent.
Brookfield Congregational Church Choir.
Ned Sperry, building committee chairperson, Fort Atkinson.
Arthur E. Waterman, architect, Fort Atkinson.
George Jakoubek, representing the T. S. Willis Company, Janesville.
Thorpe Merriman, Fairhaven board president, Fort Atkinson.
Clarence N. Peck, Fairhaven board secretary-treasurer, Whitewater.

Crawford Thayer, representing Wisconsin Congregational Laymen, Fort Atkinson.

William B. Smith, representing Wisconsin Congregational Laymen, Madison.

Mrs. Melvin Frank, representing Wisconsin Congregational Laywomen, LaCrosse.

Robert Jacobson, representing Wisconsin Congregational Youth, Milwaukee.

Administrator-chaplain Olm introduced Mrs. Genevieve Spradling, Sparta, Wisconsin, a resident-to-be, who spoke in behalf of future residents. She was over 80 years of age and wore a bright red dress. Mrs. Spradling was the "hit" of the celebration, setting a tone for future residency.

OPEN HOUSE

On June 23, 1963, an Open House attracted over 2,000 attendees. Residents opened the doors of their apartments and welcomed visitors. Much pride was exhibited by residents as they readily showed their new homes to all who wanted to see them. Common facilities [offices, lounges, kitchen/dining room, laundries, maintenance areas, beauty shop, recreation areas, library, resident storage lockers, indoor garages, etc.] were all on public display. There were no formal ceremonies, but coffee and tea was served to all who came. Eighteen gallons of coffee and 4,000 cookies were consumed. The auxiliary, sponsor of the event, provided 20 hosts and hostesses. It was considered a hugh success.

DEDICATION AND OPEN HOUSE

The home had no area large enough to accommodate those who were expected to attend the September 8, 1963, Dedication Service and Open House. The local United Church of Christ offered use of its building, but anticipated numbers would have been more than two or three times the seating capacity of the church.

Arrangements were made with the City of Whitewater to use the baseball diamond area at Starin Park, directly across the road from the Fairhaven grounds. It was a beautiful sunshine day. The sun had also shone on the three previous special events [Groundbreaking, Cornerstone Laying, and the previous Open House.]

The outdoor dedication services would have been a disaster had it rained, for attendees not only sat on the hundreds of folding chairs provided, but also on the grassy hill under the trees. A loud speaker system

provided adequate audio service. More than 1,200 persons were in attendance.

It was a glorious service with leadership represented from across the
state and nation as follows:

> Jess H. Norenberg, former conference superintendent, New
> York, who brought the message entitled "God's Great
> Design".
> Lee W. Rockwell, General Secretary of the United Church of
> Christ Council on Health and Welfare [now Council for
> Health and Human Service Ministries,] New York, who
> brought greetings from the denomination.
> Clarence F. McCall, Wisconsin Conference United Church of
> Christ Conference Minister, Madison, who spoke on behalf
> of the conference.
> Liturgists were:
> Kendrick Strong, pastor, First Congregational Church-United
> Church of Christ, Janesville, and moderator of the confer-
> ence.
> Egon E. Schieler, pastor of Our Saviour's United Church of
> Christ, Ripon, and member of the executive committee of the
> conference board and a member of the Fairhaven board.
> The choirs of First Congregational Church-United Church of
> Christ, Madison, and of Congregational Church-United
> Church of Christ, Whitewater.
> William E. Haworth, representing the residents, Whitewater.
> Participants in the presentation of the keys were:
>
> T. S. Willis, general contractor, Janesville.
> Arthur E. Waterman, architect, Fort Atkinson.
> Ned Sperry, building committee chairperson, Fort Atkinson.
> Thorpe Merriman, president of the Fairhaven Board of Directors,
> Fort Atkinson.

OTHER EVENTS

In subsequent years, there were other special events held to com-
memorate milestones and achievements. These continued to provide
public exposure for Fairhaven. Details regarding these events will be
recorded in *Fairhaven: God's Mighty Oak — The Development of the
Fairhaven Ministry — The First Three Decades — Volume II.*

Fifth Anniversary Celebration.

Flagpole Dedication.
Tenth Anniversary Celebration.
Fifteen Anniversary Celebration
Avenue of Flags Dedication.
Twentieth Anniversary Celebration.
Twenty-fifth Anniversary Celebration.
Dedication and Open House of Building AA and the CC addition.
Dedication of Building 2 D addition.
Dedication of Building 2 E addition.

TOUR GROUPS

Bus loads of people from all over the state and nation arrived regularly. Church-related tour groups from Europe [Germany and England] came. Most of the bus tours were from conference local congregations [Women's Fellowships, youth groups, circles, couples clubs, etc.] Many service clubs came: Kiwanis, Rotary, Optimist, Lions. Bus loads came from other retirement homes, senior citizens groups, high school and university students, business and professional clubs, women's clubs, etc. During the early years, it was not uncommon for one to two buses to come per week.

Various boards and/or committees came to hold meetings and tour Fairhaven. i.e. Conference Board of Directors, association entities, county agencies, local city clubs, youth groups, catechism classes, Sunday School pupils, students from high school and University of Wisconsin - Whitewater, groups of physicians, groups of attorneys, etc.

Individual carloads came — some made appointments, others came unannounced. All were accommodated. The frequency of visitors presented personnel and logistic problems. This was "home" for the residents and their privacy and life style had to be preserved. Staff arranged to use different routes, through different areas, visiting only apartments where residents agreed to participate. Tribute is given to the many residents who showed their apartments, answered questions and gave open, positive declaration of their life at Fairhaven. One of the greatest publicity assets Fairhaven had was the residents. Their eyes sparkled, their enthusiasm effervesced, and their neatness, class, and stature captivated. How could anyone believe they were anything but happy?

THE AUXILIARY

Just after Fairhaven began operating, the Auxiliary was established. A nominating committee composed of Viola Humphrey, Whitewater,

Helen Robison, Lake Geneva, and Isabel Elder, Madison, named Mary
Henningsen for the first presidency. Mary, as the first president, led the
effort to give birth to this organization. Other officers elected were: Mrs.
Kenneth Begkin, Madison, vice-president; Mrs. Karl Wickstrom, Lake
Geneva, secretary; Mrs. Elmer Rumpf, Milton, treasurer; Miss Florence
Goodhue, Whitewater, corresponding secretary. Named to the board of
directors were: Mrs. Fred Lee, Waukesha; Mrs. Walker Wyman,
Whitewater; Mrs. E.R. Hollander, Appleton; Mrs. O. J. Gates, Fort
Atkinson; and Mrs. G. L. Arbuthnot, Janesville.

   Over 560 people became charter members. First Congregational
Church-United Church of Christ, Appleton, led the way with 150 members, followed by Eau Claire First with 64, Janesville with 37, LaCrosse
with 41, Whitewater with 32, and Genoa City with 19.

   The auxiliary was designed to be a vehicle through which positive
publicity would be generated for Fairhaven, by which resident recruitment would be assisted, and by which volunteers for service at Fairhaven
would be encouraged. The auxiliary was specifically not designed as a
money making organization. Without a doubt, the auxiliary, with member
representation throughout the state, accomplished [and continues to
accomplish] its purposes for being. The following served as presidents
during the first three decades:

Mrs. Victor E. Henningsen [Mary]	1963-1966
Mrs. William F. Edge [Cynthia]	1966-1968
Mrs. Walter C. Janisch [Muriel]	1968-1970
Mrs. E. A. Fellwock [Fern]	1970-1972
Mrs. Fred Lee [Maurene]	1972-1974
Mrs. Donald Barney [Eugenia]	1974-1976
Mrs. E. A. Fellwock [Fern]	1976-1978
Mrs. William Bullamore [Isabelle]	1978-1980
Mrs. Victor E. Henningsen [Mary]	1980-1982
Mrs. John Misener [Lillian]	1982-1984
Mrs. William J. Willis [Doris]	1984-1986
Mrs. G. L. Conners [Shirley]	1986-1988

[Resigned because of illness. Vice-president presided.]
Mrs. Wayne K. Hinkle [Beth]   1988- 1990

WORD OF MOUTH

   One of the most subtle and yet effective methods of public relations
is word of mouth. Most individuals who were exposed to Fairhaven were
convinced of its worth and ready to tell others about it. What happened

could be likened to the word of mouth support that was generated when the Boston Braves moved to Milwaukee and became the Milwaukee Braves. The ball club did not have to do much advertising because almost everyone was talking about the team, the players, the great experience of seeing a major league ball game. So it was with Fairhaven. "Have you heard about the class act the Congregationalists are developing in Whitewater for older people?"

Once the general public was educated about the Fairhaven concepts, specially those who initially had difficulty understanding why a front end founders fee was charged, they became vehicles of promotion. For example: A man from southeastern Wisconsin made an appointment with the administrator-chaplain. His opening remarks were: "I am ashamed and embarrassed! I was one who vocally criticized Fairhaven for what I thought was charging an enormous founders fee for residents. But recently I drove my car from Wisconsin to California and back. Intentionally, I routed my trip so that many retirement facilities could be visited. In all I visited 15 homes. Now I am here to apologize to you and to bring you a substantial gift [a large contribution of stock] because on my entire trip I did not find one facility of comparable quality that was more reasonable in resident rates than Fairhaven. I have been educated and I am now proud to be a vocal supporter of this ministry."

Even your enemies will rise up and praise you!

NATIONAL EMPHASIS

In the early 1960's and the decade that followed, America became more and more conscious of the ever increasing numbers of citizens over 65 years of age and of their special needs. In the Asian culture, the aged are revered and respected. This is not necessarily true in American culture. However, suddenly everyone seemed to be identifying with the changes which Americans were experiencing in attitudes and knowledge about God's older children. The public was almost forced to take notice, for within 10 years the numbers of American citizens over 100 years of age grew from under 1,000 to over 10,000. Likewise, the total numbers of retirees jumped by the millions, until the older generation became one of the most powerful political influences in the country. There were nine million people over 65 years of age in 1960. They increased to 25 and one-half million by 1980 and to 30 million by 1990. Older people were anticipating the "golden years" and were expecting enhancement of life in their latter days. The United States Government recognized all these happenings and by 1972 the first White House Conference on the Aging was called into session by President Richard Nixon.

It was during this time, when the nation was giving general and specific attention to the elderly, that Fairhaven was in the most crucial stages of its development. Every time the newspaper, the radio, a magazine, a television program, a conference focused on the graying of America, it made the publicizing of Fairhaven that much easier. The development of the project could not have come during a better national climate.

FUND RAISING

Fund raising efforts for Fairhaven were the responsibility of the conference until the facility was in operation. During that time the board of directors and administrator-chaplain simply assisted the conference leadership in promotional capacities.

The Capital Funds Drive, initiated and implemented by the conference, officially closed December 31, 1963. Throughout 1962 and 1963, $286,978.28 was credited to the fund drive. This should not be viewed as an almost successful attempt at raising $300,000 Included in this sum was all the benevolent money received before June 1, 1962, when the $300,000 drive first commenced. Also included in it were all yearly allotment monies allocated to Fairhaven by the Wisconsin Congregational Conference at the end of 1962 [at the time of the merger] and the new conference's United Conference Appeal payments made in 1963 [contributed not only from Congregational church members, but also from members of the former Evangelical and Reformed churches.]

1963 giving to Fairhaven by local churches, church groups and individuals totaled $157,217.23. [$30,000 was received in 1963 as budgeted from the new United Church of Christ conference.]

[Note: Techniques used by conference officials in attacking fund raising during the pre-construction and construction periods are described in the chapter "The Financing".]

The conference designated Mother's Day [Festival of the Christian Home] Sunday 1962 as a time for all congregations to hold a special offering for Fairhaven. In anticipation of that offering, advanced publicity was addressed. Four multi-colored brochures were written by the administrator-chaplain, edited by conference officials, with design by Congregationalist Peter Millner of Lake Geneva. Thirty thousand copies of each of the four brochures were delivered to Whitewater for distribution to the churches throughout the state. The brochures had to be counted out for allotment to each congregation, per membership size, repackaged and then delivered to the various communities. Volunteers to complete this task were solicited from the Congregational Church, Whitewater. Ten banquet tables were placed in the gymnasium of the church [lower half of which is now the church's fellowship hall — upper half is now classrooms.] One hundred twenty thousand brochures were stacked on these tables and it took three days to get them properly counted, packaged and ready for distribution.

Administrator-chaplain Olm looked at the 120,000 brochures, stacked so high on so many tables and received an insight into the conference's task. Two and one-half one dollar bills would have to be placed along side of each brochure, if the fund drive goals were to be met, for the conference was attempting to raise $300,000. Such a fund raising effort was unprecedented in conference history. "Oh my! Could this really be done?"

Cars and trucks carried the bundles to association meetings and/or to local churches. Gold colored offering envelopes were printed and distributed separately to the churches. Unfortunately, the Mother's Day offerings contributed only a small portion of the fund drive income. Most of the contributions were raised when congregations borrowed from local banks and forwarded the cash to the conference or Fairhaven and then the local church paid off the loan over three [or whatever] years. [See Chapter "The Financing".]

LEGACIES

Additional comment about legacies is appropriate. Congregationalists responded to Conference Superintendent Norenberg's repeated requests to remember Fairhaven in their wills. Almost all the legacies received over the first three decades came from church members who deemed the ministry worthy of support and from residents who experienced life at Fairhaven. Hundreds of thousands of dollars were inherited. These dollars were used for capital purposes: purchase of furnishings, redecoration, payments toward indebtedness. On many occasions, the legacies helped to alleviate financial strain or to assist in keeping Fairhaven a first class operation. However, not all legacies came from Congregationalists. For example: One day a person, who was not a Congregationalist, living in a community 50 miles away, phoned the administrator-chaplain and said, "I have been watching the development of the Fairhaven program and I like what I see. Currently, I am constructing my will and I want to remember Fairhaven in it. I have a few questions to ask of you." Years later, after this person's death, a very large inheritance — the largest legacy recorded in the first three decades — was received by Fairhaven. May the glory be to God!

GOD KNOWS EXACTLY WHAT WE NEED

Stresses and strains — specially the financial ones — reared ugly heads often during the development of Fairhaven. The magnitude of the program and limited resources to get the job done were contributing causes. While considerable faith was exercised during these pressure times, more could have been practiced. While patience was practiced, more patience could have been generated.

Impatience and lack of faith can be the beginning of all sorts of problems. This holds true of individuals, corporations, and of mission projects. Running ahead of God or trying to force God's hand breeds many kinds of problems. But God's timing is perfect. At just the right time, God provides the solutions to our problems, the answers to our needs.*1 Through legacies these truths were experienced time and time again. Since in the "fullness of time" God gave Jesus Christ, the Son, that coming is the guarantee that God knows exactly what we need and when we need it.

> God did not keep back [God's] own Son, but. . .gave him for us. If God did this, won't [God] freely give us everything else? [Romans 8:32.]

This was clearly demonstrated through Fairhaven's being the recipient of legacies — often at just the right time.

The "water" generated from publicity and fund raising gave nourishment for the fledgling oak tree.

*1 From *Today*, April 15, 1997. Copyright permission from the Back to God Hour.

CHAPTER VII

The Site and The Buildings

"Mighty oaks from little acorns grow."
Early Fairhaven brochure

Arthur E. Waterman, Waterman, Fuge & Associates, Fort Atkinson, Wisconsin, was the architect of Fairhaven. What a blessing he was! The husband of Margaret, father of Robert and Susie, ardent Congregationalist, humble and modest, personable, intelligent, benevolent, sensitive, quiet mannered, and community minded — Art Waterman was all of those things! To the developers of Fairhaven, he was a mainstay — a rock of assurance, a confidant, and a friend. He exemplified his faith in his person and in his profession. Art Waterman was living proof that you did not have to go to the big cities and large firms to solicit quality. In 1970 he was elected to

Arthur E. Waterman - 1972

the Fairhaven Board of Directors, became president of the board in 1974 and entered residency, with his wife, Margaret, on August 25, 1989. He received the Honor Award for Meritorious Service on July 8, 1972.

Since Art Waterman was a staunch member of First Congregational Church, Fort Atkinson, he had special, personal interest in and commitment to the Fairhaven project. He worked with conference leadership in trying to develop concept and philosophy as the "home-to-be" was being contemplated. His involvement in these matters proved to be helpful. He drew building plans that tried to incorporate the proper concept and philosophy into construction. The abstract had to evolve into the physical. Later, when the home was in operation, it became easier to bring this focus to further visibility by developing image and setting practical living patterns, reflecting the Christian faith. The physical structures blended

The Site—1961 at upper left center in the middle of the block. Church with spire in lower left is Congregational Church (now Congregational Church United Church of Christ.) Upper left and center open space is Starin Park.

with Christian concept and philosophy. Theology became visibly manifested.

In the initial stages of development, the most significant abstract idea was most generally accepted by Congregationalists, but not so well appreciated by others. It centered in the strong desire to emphasize residency rather than institutionalism. For if the Fairhaven ministry was to be successful in the breaking out of the traditional medical and institutional molds, it was imperative that the physical environment lend itself to that goal. To this, Architect Waterman devoted his resources. It is easier for someone to achieve this type goal when money expenditure is no issue. Fairhaven leaders did not have such luxury. Architect Waterman was fully aware that Wisconsin Congregational Conference had not only initiated the largest program in the history of the Wisconsin churches, but initiated it in the faith that somehow the finances for the project would materialize. Everything the architect did reflected thorough consideration of cost. That added an additional burden and greater dedication to the task.

THE SITE

Viola Humphrey, long time loyal Congregationalist, had read in Church Life that the Wisconsin Congregational Conference was urging local church members to submit suggestions for site location of the proposed "community for the aging."

Heywood and Viola Humphrey's home and property abutted a nearly ten acre parcel of land that lay unused in the center of a long city block, near downtown Whitewater.

One day, Viola was washing breakfast dishes. She looked over her kitchen sink through the kitchen windows and focused on that unused piece of property. Viola said to herself, "This would make an ideal location for the conference's 'community for the aging.' Why should it not be built in Whitewater? I'm going to suggest that this site be considered by the conference."

Subsequently, Viola talked to her pastor, the Rev. Donald S. Hobbs, and asked him to write to the conference superintendent for her. Mr. Hobbs did just that. The conference leaders inspected the site. Later, the conference voted that the Whitewater site would be the place where the "home" would be built.

The conference decided to accept the Whitewater location, contingent on cooperation from the City of Whitewater and acquisition of the property. Conference leaders, including Jess Norenberg and William Bradford Smith, negotiated with city officials in regard to property tax exemption, zoning matters, infra-structure, etc. They negotiated with

Oromel H. and Lutie N. Bigelow, who owned the west one-half of the site the conference was trying to obtain. They also negotiated with Ben and Evelyn McCauley, who owned the east one-half of the site and a connected lot, with a ranch home fronting on 244 N. Park Street.

Since the Bigelows were members of the Congregational Church, Whitewater, Jess Norenberg and William Bradford Smith contacted them first about possible land sale to the conference. Initially, the Bigelows were hesitant about selling their property. The McCauleys were visited and they expressed interest, if the conference was willing to purchase the 244 N. Park Street house along with the land.

It was ironic that Ben McCauley, a Roman Catholic, was the catalyst in persuading the Congregational Bigelows to sell the land to the conference. He convinced them it was the right thing to do.

Purchase of the 244 N. Park Street house was not a burden for the conference. It had been decided that the clergyperson, who would be engaged to operate the "home," would be required to live in this adjacent house. It was called "the parsonage." Close geographic proximity to the "home" for the "manager" proved advantageous to the program, not only during the construction period, but also for nearly three decades of administration that followed.

The City of Whitewater did not have a certified survey of the nearly ten acres that the conference purchased. Immediately, Batterman surveyors of Beloit, Wisconsin, were engaged to complete a survey at the cost of over $1,000. City officials said the copy of the survey given to the city was one of the few certified surveys that the city had on file.

A part of Fairhaven's success should be credited to the excellent Whitewater site, which met concept and philosophical specifications. Three factors were involved. While the selectors of the site were not fully cognizant of these factors when the site selection was voted, they became aware of them as the project developed.

First, the site fulfilled eleven of twelve requirements for a retirement facility location, as set forth by the Architect's Research Guild of California. No longer were older people destined to become isolated in the country. Located in the "heart" of a residential section of the city, residents would easily be able to do their shopping and participate in community affairs. Downtown Whitewater and the Wisconsin State University [now University of Wisconsin - Whitewater] are only a few blocks away from the site. A large well-supervised city park [Starin Park] is across the street. The Whitewater public library was at the end of the block. Five churches were within two blocks. The only requirement the site did not fulfill was that it was not within geographic proximity to light industry, where residents could participate in part time employment.

Local citizens had called the site "the pasture" because horses were left to roam in it. No future resident was going out to pasture, if the innovative concept was to be realized.

Second, if one would take a map and draw a circle with a fifty mile radius around Whitewater, that circle would embrace 80% of all the congregations affiliated with the Wisconsin Congregational Conference. From that perspective, Whitewater seemed ideally located. The conference was interested in serving its own constituency, as well as others. After the formulation of the United Church of Christ, when the former Evangelical and Reformed churches were included, a circle of 100 mile radius had to be drawn to include 80% of the new conference congregations.

Third, in the early 1960's, the University of Wisconsin Extension service conducted a survey to determine the migration patterns of Wisconsin people who retired after 65 years of age. The survey discovered that those who retired were migrating from the north and west to the south and east. They were not going to the urban centers and they avoided the rural locations. Predominantly, the migration was to small communities. Whitewater's population [7,000 to 12,000 over three decades] met the small city classification and it was directly in the northwest to southeast migration pattern.

Furthermore, in the late 1950's and early 1960's, Whitewater was known as a community that attracted [for residency] retired farmers and company sales representatives. Representatives of companies found Whitewater to be strategically located for their needs. They could market their products by using the "wagon wheel" approach, and thus spend more evenings at home with their families. Hence, even before the conference "home" was involved, Whitewater's location attracted retirees and, via sales representatives, proved itself to be a geographic center for southeastern Wisconsin.

The site proved to be an architectural challenge. The five buildings had to be located to take advantage of the elongated middle-of-the-block tract. Three buildings were constructed in V shapes to reduce the length of the corridors. Not only was the site narrow and long, it also sloped considerably from the south to the north. On the north end, a small creek wound its way, west to east, around a large clump of willow trees, across the narrow width of the property. The south one-half of the site had very little soil over bedrock. Bedrock was so close to the surface that no basements were proposed for Buildings D and E, which were the most southerly located.

Crawl tunnels [about four feet high] were constructed around the foundations of Buildings D and E. These tunnels facilitated utility pipes and created an insulation buffer, so that floors of the apartments would not be cold during the winter season. The strategy proved successful, for after nearly three decades of residency, not one complaint about cold floors was received.

The sloping terrain problem was partially alleviated by having the site graded, removing soil from the south end and depositing it on the north end. Final compensation for the slope was made when the architect planned for each of the five buildings to be erected one foot lower in grade than the previous building. The southern most building [Building E] was constructed first. After construction, the floor of Building E had a four foot higher grade than the floor of Building A. Plans included lower levels [improved and decorated basements] for Buildings A, B and C. Soil borings indicated there was sufficient excavation room to create these lower levels. However, it was necessary to blast bedrock for one-third of Building C [south end] in order to construct a full lower level for Building C. During excavation for Building C, construction workers uncovered a strong flowing underground spring. This spring had to be harnessed and kept under control or the Building C lower level would be continuously flooded. Two sump pumps were installed, one "back-stopping" the other. These pumps continue to regulate the spring, even to this day.

One hundred and two caissons were drilled and poured for the foundations of Buildings A and B. Each one is 24 inches in diameter and is filled with concrete to bedrock, the level of which varies from 11 to 16 feet below the surface.

In later years, four acquisitions of land adjacent to the site were negotiated:

First, a strip of land embracing more than one-half of a city lot was purchased from Clark and Thelma Rockwell, Congregationalists and adjoining neighbors of Fairhaven, to provide driveway access to North Franklin Street. This land was purchased and then immediately donated to Fairhaven on October 5, 1962, by Victor and Mary Henningsen, Milwaukee, in memory of Mary Henningsen's mother, Mrs. W. P. Roseman, former Whitewater resident. The drive was designated Roseman Memorial Drive. Seven feet of additional land beyond the one-half lot was donated by the Elwin B. Rockwell family in memory of Mrs. Hazel M. Rockwell.

Second, two city lots on North Park Street, owned by James and Joan Andersen, were acquired. This ground was utilized for resident garden plots.

Third, the home owned by Oromel and Lutie Bigelow was purchased from the Bigelow estate. This acquisition provided driving and walking access to Main Street, Whitewater.

Fourth, the former First Christian Science Church, located on North Franklin Street, with the back end of the property abutting the Fairhaven grounds, was purchased when the congregation placed the property on the market.

THE BUILDINGS

Architect Waterman and the soon-to-be "manager" [the Rev. Carroll J. Olm] of the soon-to-be "home" met at the Groundbreaking service that was conducted at Congregational Church [now Congregational Church-United Church of Christ], Whitewater, on Sunday, October 2, 1960. Those attending walked in parade fashion from the church to the site for the completion of the ceremonies. The two men walked together, leading the procession. During that walk, they discussed the future "home" design and project function. It was emphasized by Mr. Olm that the central four story building [Building C] had to be designed in a manner that would facilitate conversion of the residential apartments into supportive care living units. His thought was that residents might need such service in the future. Gradually, this took place. Three decades later, almost all initial residential apartments in Building C were transformed into supportive care areas. All of the second floor embraced skilled nursing rooms and therapy areas. While all of third floor was licensed for skilled care, its functional use was [and continues to be] intermediate level care. The fourth floor, with all residential apartments at Fairhaven, was licensed for C. B. R. F. [Community Based Residential Facility] level service. All apartments at Fairhaven are licensed for C. B. R. F. This level of service may be administered throughout the facility in apartments, without residents having to be transferred to another location within the facility. Since nursing staff was heavily concentrated on Building C floors two and three, it became a natural flow to have residents who needed the highest level of C. B. R. F. care to locate on fourth floor. It was identified as "Residency Plus." This same development occurred on third floor prior to its being licensed for skilled nursing and intermediate care.

Two decades after the Groundbreaking ceremonies, most of Building C had developed into a more than independent residency care area. Those who administered the care were grateful that the architect had drawn plans that facilitated converting the Building C apartments into service care units.

Initially, each of the five buildings was designed to be free standing [no interconnecting walkways]. This was consistent with the "preserva-

Under Construction—1962 L-R: Buildings E, D, C, B and A. The house at lower right is the Fairhaven parsonage. Upper left and center is Wisconsin State University (Now University of Wisconsin—Whitewater.)

tion of independence" concept. Wisconsin winters considered, it made sense to the administrator-chaplain that the buildings should be interconnected. The architect was amiable to the idea, but it took a considerable period of time to convince conference leadership. Undoubtedly, the additional construction cost factor, generated by the addition of four enclosed walkways, weighed heavily on the conference superintendent. Benefits derived by residents more than justified the cost.

Another issue developed when the architect, in an attempt to reduce capital expenditures, suggested that the lower levels of Buildings A and B be eliminated. The question was asked, "What are you going to do with all that undesignated space?" The answer was, "We will use it all and more, if it's available." Soon after operations began, all three lower levels were fully utilized. They embraced a library, beauty shop, employee lounge, activities room, carpentry shop, a large area for weaving looms, an exercise room, a game and recreation area, individual storage lockers for each apartment and resident garages. [Accommodations were always made for special interests or needs. For a period of time a special area was designated for photography developing and another for working with stained glass. Still another housed a kiln for baking ceramic creations.] Later, a conference room and the warmly accepted and highly publicized indoor garden, with adjacent park and plant nursery, was developed. For a time, a portion of the lower level of Building C was used for the bookkeeping staff.

Initially, all the apartment storage lockers were designed to be located in the lower level of Building C. After designers were convinced that residents would use an activities room, the library, the beauty shop, etc. daily, the apartment storage lockers were relocated farther from the elevators, in the lower level of Building B. Later, more lockers for residents were provided on the south side of the lower level of Building A.

DESIGN CONSIDERATIONS

Many considerations were incorporated in the design of the buildings. In the early 1960's most of them were considered innovative. Three decades later most of them are accepted as something expected. Among them were safety factors, aesthetics, durability, limitations of the elderly, comfort for residents and, of course, keeping faithful to concept and philosophy.

Safety Factors: One of the most feared threats to the safety of the elderly is fire. For that reason, almost all the construction materials used were considered either fire proof or highly fire resistant. Concrete was used for the floors and ceilings. Every square foot of ceiling and floor paneling weighs 65 pounds. Each of the 26 four story concrete beams for

Building C, pre-cast in one piece, weigh three and one-half tons. Interior walls feature pyrobar, metal studs and fire resistant plaster board. The basic structure contains no wood.

A state of the art control system was installed for fire alarms. Water hoses [now no longer used] and two types of extinguishers were strategically placed per code. Grab bars were installed in all toilet and bath areas. No steps were used, except in the emergency exits in the five story Building C and at the lower level exterior exits.

Aesthetics: The buildings were designed in the contemporary concept of architecture. Exterior walls featured white grooved pre-cast concrete panels, interspersed under the windows with gray-black aggregate stone panels.

Original Main Lounge and Chapel

Radke Studio

The main lounge and dining room were made attractive with initial decor of light gold walls, structured accents of aqua, with aqua carpeting and drapery to match. Watermelon pink cushioned dining room walnut captain's chairs matched the color of a mural that decorated the north dining room wall. Five other lounges were placed strategically throughout the buildings so residents could enjoy easy accessibility to them.

Seven feet wide corridors reduced any possible feelings of confinement.

Durability and Maintenance: Almost no exterior painting became necessary since construction was pre-cast concrete. Every decade, the exterior caulking had to be upgraded and periodically the roofing needed attention. Otherwise, the exterior was long lasting, maintenance free. Little structural attention was ever needed on the interior. The buildings were built solid – to endure. If changes were to be made which affected the structure, it was more difficult to accomplish because it is so hard to remove concrete. Through the years, considerable numbers of dollars were saved by the corporation because the buildings are so durable and maintenance free.

Limitations of the Elderly: This consideration was a foremost one in the mind of Architect Waterman. Since the buildings were designed for residents and were being built for residents, residents' limitations and special needs had to be given first priority.

Though the five buildings were on different grade levels, one can go through the main entrance and then ambulate to any extremity of the facility without going out of doors or climbing a stair. Elevators were strategically placed for access to higher or lower stories.

Heights of windows, height of electrical outlets, types of lighting, heights of emergency stair steps, heights of toilet stools and vanities, etc., were all factors to accommodate the residents' needs.

Comfort: Since each older person has a personal comfort level temperature wise, each room was equipped with separate thermostatic control. Sound control was considered when resilient clips, along with plaster board, pyrobar and dead air space were installed between apartments. It greatly reduced sound penetration. Apartment and lounge picture windows were placed as low as structurally possible for maximum exterior viewing.

Concept and Philosophy: Of the original 102,000 square feet of space in the facility, 47,000 square feet was utilized for 115 apartments. It was the architectural plan to make Fairhaven as non-institutional as possible, so that the philosophy of the conference could be expressed in the buildings as well as in the management.

Consistent with the thrust of residency rather than institutionalism, six different styles of apartments were introduced, partly for variety and partly to meet the financial capability of residents. Initially, no corridor hand rails were installed, avoiding institutionalization. Later, when rails were needed, residential looking hand rails were incorporated.

All apartments had private baths, with tubs and shower heads, adequate storage space, kitchenettes with garbage disposals, electric ranges and refrigerator/freezers. There were TV and telephone outlets and more than ample electrical outlets.

After more than three decades of service, the Fairhaven buildings continue to be structurally sound, relatively maintenance free, and appear to be new. Administration continuously addresses upgrading and redecoration needs. As a result, Fairhaven remains competitive with newly constructed retirement facilities.

Cleanliness: The buildings were designed so that it was easy to keep them clean. Over the years, one of the distinctive features of Fairhaven was its cleanliness. Frequently, people remark about Fairhaven's cleanliness. No chipped paint. No dust or dirt. No foul odors. Employees were trained to be observant — to see the little things that needed attention — specially in regard to continued housekeeping. Things cannot always be new, but they can be clean. Special attention was also given to exterior grounds. While it was always a challenge to keep the trees trimmed, the grass cut, and the flower and shrub beds free from weeds, it was done. Special praise and credit to the housekeeping and maintenance employees!

GENERAL CONTRACTOR

Fairhaven was blessed by contracting with the general contractors, T. S. Willis Company of Janesville, Wisconsin. A decision was made by the conference and T. S. Willis Company that a negotiated contract would be mutually beneficial. This negotiated contract negated the bidding process. It permitted the owner to pick the contractor of choice and work together with that contractor to construct quality buildings, while establishing reasonable financial parameters and other safeguards, mutually agreed upon during budget development. There was a maximum level of profit the contractor could earn. Any savings, over and above that level, reverted to the owner. Costs were guaranteed not to exceed the amounts established in the contract. Regular meetings were held at least weekly to coordinate administrative matters. In addition, the general contractor was in constant contact with the sub-contractors.

Besides Mr. T. S. Willis, four additional employees of the T. S. Willis Company contributed significantly to Fairhaven construction: George Jakoubek, Harold Swanstrom, Gordon Day and later Johnny Link.

Hyland, Hall Company and H. & H. Electric Company, Madison, were the mechanical contractors, doing the heating, electrical, plumbing, ventilation and air-conditioning work.

PROPHETIC QUESTION MARKS

During construction, a few local Whitewater citizens made comments which in retrospect are humorous:

At the time the exterior walls were being erected, a Whitewater Congregationalist confronted the administrator-chaplain with the "cheering??" remark, "What in the world are you trying to do over there? It looks like you're building a bunch of chicken coops." By early 1963 the person who made the comment was living in one of those "chicken coops."

One evening the administrator-chaplain's phone rang. It was one of Fairhaven's neighbors, who had some building talent. He was convinced that the roof line of Building E, then under construction, was exceedingly low and he warned that residents-to-be would be bumping their heads on the ceilings. The architect was notified. He changed nothing. Of course — facetiously — all the residents of first floor Building E are bumping their heads on the ceiling.

Local Whitewater citizen Dr. Charles E. Morphew related that he refuted remarks from several persons who predicted that Fairhaven's lower level would be continuously flooded from underground water. Of course — facetiously — everyone using the lower level needs hip boots or a row boat.

PLAUDITS OF PRAISE

Fairhaven officials believed the concept implemented at Fairhaven was innovative for Wisconsin and that the buildings were exceptional in quality, livability, and beauty. After construction was completed, their belief was confirmed by others, such as:

Dale Jennerjohn, Wisconsin State Board of Health [now Wisconsin Department of Health and Family Services] "Your home not only fulfills homes in the state requirements, but goes far beyond. You have one of the finest homes in the State of Wisconsin."

A medical doctor from Milwaukee [referring to the infirmary] "You are not only administering a home for senior citizens here — you are also administering a hospital, short of surgery. This is wonderful!"

George Hall of Hyland, Hall Company, Madison - ". . . . .We have few jobs as satisfying as this one was."

Construction foreman - "I travel five states for my company and there's not another home equal in construction or beauty to this one. You've got something to be proud of."

John Gaelestle, engineer - "In the 53 years of my building experience I have not seen a building that is constructed in a finer way than Fairhaven."

Radke Studio

The completed five original buildings—1963, L-R Buildings A, B, C, D and E.

T. S. Willis, general contractor - "Long after any monetary considerations are forgotten, I will always consider the building of Fairhaven as the high point in the more than half-century of my activity in the building business."

At the conclusion of construction, the architect and builders joined the conference pastors and congregations in giving the glory to God.

The Rev. Robert Midgley, minister of Central Union Church, Honolulu, Hawaii, wrote a letter to Architect Waterman on February 5, 1976:

How I remember those days when we all participated together in digging the first spadeful of dirt for the building of Fairhaven. And your work on the planning of the building was truly a masterpiece of professionalism. As a Christian layman you grasped entirely what we wanted in the way of a building and the concept. Wisconsin will be eternally grateful to you for the skills that you had to match with the needs of the conference. . . .[Note: Robert Midgley was pastor of Lake Edge Congregational Church, Madison, and the moderator of the Wisconsin Congregational Conference the year the Groundbreaking ceremonies were held.]

SPECIAL NOTE: In 1996, Architect Waterman, past 90 years of age, was transferred from his Fairhaven residential apartment to a private room in Fairhaven's skilled nursing section. There he reflected on the work he had so skillfully accomplished in the construction of Fairhaven. He said,

"I did buildings in the midwest, in New York, in the south. I built bridges, but I class this — Fairhaven — as my favorite. I enjoyed the Fairhaven project. This was an experimental building. I tried something new — concrete panels, factory built — and stone block walls, covered with plaster. There they are! [36 years later.] No cracks!

"We have lived through an interesting era. So many new/innovative things were tried and proved to be successful. We took chances, but it worked out. Architects still come here and take good looks.

"I was bound into a budget and couldn't do everything I wanted to do, but the buildings held up very well. I'm comfortable with what we did. People seem to be happy with it. People are happy living here."

Then Mr. Waterman's head turned and his eyes focused on the big burr oak tree standing majestically outside his window. With a far off look and a bit of moisture in his eyes, he started to sing —

O love that wilt not let me go. . . . .

It was an endearing happening. How often does a 90 year old person burst out singing in your presence? In this case, not really bursting, but spontaneously expressing emotions on the significance of God's love and faithfulness in the accomplishments of the past. The voice was soft, measured and slightly raspy —

I rest my weary soul in thee. . . . .

It was as if he were dipping down into the reservoir of God's grace and finding there the real substance of life and the assurance of eternal providence.

I give thee back the life I owe. . . . .

Nothing pretentious — just serene, quiet, almost introvert willingness to trust in the Almighty and to allow that aura of God's love, kindness, grace to enfold him.

That in thine ocean depths its flow
May richer, fuller be.

Perhaps a visitor from Illinois caught and embraced that spiritual insight when he said, "Fairhaven is a Christian gem. Always keep it that way."

A mighty oak had taken root!

[Note: Art Waterman died peacefully on September 19, 1997. Knowing death was eminent, the Fairhaven staff suggested to Art's son and daughter that they come to see their father. Susan visited with him. A bit later Art tried to sing, but found difficulty doing so. The social services staff members arranged for Activities Worker Susan Harris to come to the room to sing a few hymns, among which were "Amazing Grace" and "How Great Thou Art." In a low voice Art whispered, "I'm so glad I built this place." Son Robert was with his father when God called him.

> I give thee back the life I owe. . . . .
> That in thine ocean depths its flow
> May richer, fuller be.]

CHAPTER VIII

The Residents

"The eternal God is [your] refuge, and
underneath are the everlasting arms."
Deuteronomy 33:27 KJV

The early residents were "the salt of the earth." Their faith, their vision, their love, their personalities, their character set a tone that sent the Fairhaven program spinning off into levels of quality the founders had not dared to believe possible. The early residents were a diverse group of individuals with varied backgrounds and with histories reflecting a pleasing variety of social, economic, and cultural levels. Some had the benefit of higher education and professional careers. Some had little schooling, but shared the wealth of their knowledge attained through the "school of life." A few were considered fiscally well to-do. All of them were wealthy in other ways. Those who were less fortunate financially never found that to be a barrier. To a great extent, this same balance occurred throughout the first three decades of Fairhaven's history and probably will continue into infinity.

Without a doubt, the first residents created an atmosphere, an image, which was priceless. They demonstrated a high level of culture — they

Residents Adolph and Josephine Pierce—1972 at C-D Entrance
Deaconess Hospital (Now Sinai Samaritan Hospital)

had dignity and they showed class. Thus a tone was set for future years and Fairhaven began to be known as a "class act."

This tone permeated into the life of the facility, into the community of Whitewater and throughout the state and nation. In practical terms, the residency was always neatly and cleanly dressed and well groomed. Some observers erroneously equated that with dollars and therefore, Fairhaven had the early reputation of being the "Whitewater Hilton," where only wealthy people resided. While these false impressions were being verbalized, the "Whitewater Hilton" was almost going bankrupt. [See Chapter "The Financing".] Contrary to those false impressions, Fairhaven targeted the middle class older person from the very beginning. One delightful early resident had no capital and a very limited monthly income. The corporation, after thorough investigation, had given her a founders fee grant to make residency possible. The same woman had dignity and self-respect, dressed neatly and was well-groomed. One day Marilyn Olm, Administrator-chaplain Olm's wife, over-heard two local citizens talking about the resident. "Look over there," said one to the other. "That's XXXXX and she lives at Fairhaven. She's a rich bitch!"

Without doubt, most of what the residents were [and are] they brought with them. Yet even older people grow — and for that reason a conscientious effort was made to take the best that each resident had to offer and "lift" that up. The good was emphasized. The not so good was suppressed as much as possible. With everyone contributing the best of their qualities came a wave of congenial atmosphere, conducive to high quality living. Gradually, what could be termed a residential philosophy developed within Fairhaven. That residential philosophy became contagious. Verbalization of this is challenging, but it must be done to adequately describe this intriguing and significantly important aspect of Fairhaven's history.

Facilities are important, but facilities alone will never make a home. There must be something additional. The additional is not found in building materials, but in the heart and life of the residency and staff of the agency. Here we talk about the intangibles. As one resident put it, "These facilities are lovely, but that's not what makes this place live. It's the unseen, the abstract, that is so important. It's in the air." Christians say it's the Holy Spirit in their midst.

The Apostle Paul wrote to the Romans:

> If our minds are ruled by the Spirit, we will have life and peace. . . People who don't have the Spirit of Christ in them don't

belong to him. But Christ dwells in you. So you are alive. . . God's Spirit now lives in you. . ." Romans 8: 9-11.

People are people — and all have "goods" and "not so goods." To emphasize the expression of the "goods" — to get the best out of every resident — lends to the creation of an atmosphere that enhances love rather than destroying it.

The motivation to love and be loved is a basic premise of the Fairhaven residential philosophy. This is expressed by Jesus, "You must love each other, just as I have loved you." [John 13:34.] While the lover is actively engaged in loving others, he/she, too, is an object of love. It must be a "two-way street," a two-fold thrust.

In a residency of elderly persons — whether that residency be ambulatory or convalescent, retirement or nursing — close interaction with other people is there. Today, independence is very effectively fostered in the newer retirement centers. Even in these there is a greater degree of social intercourse existing than that which the resident had when he/she lived in his/her own bungalow. The close proximity of neighbors provides new opportunities for positive personality expression. The resident upon admission feels a new adventure and is susceptible to new relationships and new ideas, or at least old ideas clothed in new forms. The home must get the "best" from the resident, as it gives the "best" to the resident. When the "best" is given and then acknowledged, the giver and the recipient find a newness of life. Several years ago a wonderful woman working at Dane County Home, Verona, Wisconsin, told us, "Each day everyone should do at least one thing for someone else." This thought we incorporated arbitrarily into Fairhaven's life. Every resident, every employee, was asked to do at least one thing each day, that was not required of him/her, for someone else. Boy Scouts of America use the same tack. It's the Scout law — to do a good deed every day. The incorporation of this tack in residential life results in the residents living outside of themselves. There should not be withdrawal. The resident has new dignity. The resident is doing something for someone else. He/she has purpose. Life has meaning. Whenever people concentrate their attention on others, self is not the center. Living outside of self is the secret to happy days. In essence, it is living an unselfish life style.

"But what can I do for someone else, Reverend?" the ninety years old male wheelchair resident said. "Two things, Will," came the quick reply. "You can smile at those walking past you and you can greet them with a cheery 'Hello. Isn't it a nice day?' and secondly, you can let yourself be an object of our love." He could encourage others and be an example of how a person of faith remains true to the important principles of life even though his life is fraught with problems, both physical and otherwise.

To let oneself be the object of another's love is equally important to loving others. We hear about stingy givers. What about stingy receivers? Early resident Alice Sperry, mother of Ned Sperry, who served as chair of the Fairhaven building and furnishings committee, taught the administrator-chaplain about being a stingy receiver. She spoke about stingy receivers when the administrator-chaplain was insisting that he pay her for an anniversary card she was providing. Alice Sperry contended that receiving graciously is an art to develop for worthwhile living. She was right.

Letting oneself be the object of a neighbor's love contributes to the neighbor's welfare and thereby performs a valuable service. "Why should I live any longer? My body is frail and my life is far spent," the old man said. The chaplain replied, "If you die — your children, your friends, the staff and other residents no longer have you as a recipient of love. Do you wish to take that away from them? If you are gone, a void is created until another is found to take your place. To properly function, every person must find expression of love — and love, to be love, must be received by someone or something."

A December 26, 1964, hand-written letter from the Rev. Dr. Jess H. Norenberg, the retired "father" of Fairhaven, to the administrator-chaplain, "lifts up" the practicality of this love relationship:

> My favorite memory [after visiting Fairhaven] came to me on the morning when you took me to the infirmary. In the hallway a tiny white-haired woman in a wheel chair said, "Is that you, Reverend?" She then took your hand, pressed it against her cheek, and said, "I love you." That kind of reward, worth more than silver and gold, cannot be had without a price.

RESIDENT JENNIE T. SCHRAGE

The first person to catch a glimpse into this philosophy was Miss Jennie T. Schrage of Madison, Wisconsin, for she was the first person to sign a Fairhaven residential agreement. Jennie, as everyone called her, was a member of First Congregational Church, Madison, Wisconsin, and it was through her church that she discovered Fairhaven. She knew Jess and Loretta Norenberg, William Bradford and Betty Smith, and Harold and Molly Brandenburg, all of whom were members at First Church and immersed in the Fairhaven dream. Undoubtedly, these and other friends helped Jennie to formulate her decisions. Jennie was an intelligent person and was well known throughout the state since she was employed for many years with the Wisconsin Traveling Library Association.

After a series of letters flowed between Miss Schrage and Fairhaven, the administrator-chaplain drove to Madison on January 31, 1961, to visit with her in her home. Her home was pleasantly located a few blocks west of First Church. The nervousness experienced by the administrator-chaplain, as he climbed the stairs to the second floor apartment, was soon dispelled by the friendly hostess and her cordial welcome. After considerable conversation about

Jennie T. Schrage

what Fairhaven was projected to become, the agreements were read and then signed. After three decades the administrator-chaplain still feels the excitement of the first signing and how the signing generated a heavy weight of responsibility. This resident-to-be and many others like her to follow, expected that the hopes and dreams of what they visualized for their retirement through Fairhaven would become reality. It was a strong act of faith on Jennie's part. It brought considerable focus to the importance of making certain the conference and the Fairhaven Board of Directors and administration could and would prove faithful to what was being guaranteed in the agreement. It was a weighty commitment by both Jennie and the corporation. There was satisfaction in knowing that it would not be too long before the reason for all the work and struggles would become reality. This "residency" milestone carried much more satisfaction than that generated by land acquisition, brick and mortar, legal documents, financing and fund raising.

Jennie had leased an alcove apartment located on the southwest corner of Building C's third floor. Since Jennie did not want to temporarily reside in an E or D apartment until her apartment was finished, she was not the first to reside at Fairhaven. She moved in on April 1, 1963, the seventeenth resident to arrive. On numerous occasions she testified that her faith in signing the first agreement was justified and that she experienced everything which she hoped her retirement at Fairhaven would be. Several times Jennie spoke positively about her Fairhaven residency at various churches and civic groups in Madison and elsewhere.

A small episode happened one day when Jennie was shopping in downtown Whitewater. A visitor rushed into the Fairhaven front entrance lobby shouting, "There's smoke coming out of your third floor windows." The alarms were turned on, the fire department was called, staff made immediate investigation. Thick black smoke in clouds was pouring out of Jennie Schrage's apartment. Everyone was tense and apprehensive. All the excitement dissipated when it was announced that before Jennie left for shopping she had forgotten to turn off the stove burner on which she had prunes cooking. Nothing was bruised except Jennie's dignity.

The Schrage apartment signing was publicized with articles and pictures throughout the conference. Later Jennie and her lovely apartment were featured on a Fairhaven colored post card, which was available for purchase.

IRENE LEFFINGWELL GATES

Another resident agreement signing, also a milestone, was highly publicized in the Whitewater area. A sweet, physically attractive, personable, long-standing member of the Whitewater community by the name of Irene Leffingwell came to the administrator-chaplain's home one day. She announced, "I am going to sign a Fairhaven residency agreement. I am going to take the largest apartment you offer and I'm going to live in it by myself and you are going to save me money." Administrator-chaplain Olm replied, "Mrs. Leffingwell, tell me about it because others are saying that Fairhaven is so expensive." She said, "Most people haven't taken the time to get out their pencils and figure what it costs to own and maintain their homes. Well, I have — and taking an average over the last three years, I find that I am

Irene Leffingwell Gates
Connell Studio

spending more per year than the Fairhaven founders fee pro-rated over ten years. Furthermore, my utilities are running higher than the $100 per month maintenance fee I will pay. [Since she was taking the apartment alone, she had to pay the $50 per person charge for each of two, or $100 per month. The apartment to which she referred was built to accommodate two persons.]

That was music to the ears of the administrator-chaplain, for it was considered important that Fairhaven be accepted and appreciated by the Whitewater community. This had to help. Irene Leffingwell was highly respected in Whitewater. Her late husband was a long time men's clothing store proprietor. Her son, Chap Leffingwell succeeded his father in operating the store. [At this time of writing, the store is operated by Irene's grandson Harry Leffingwell.] Irene was an influential member of the Congregational Church in Whitewater. For decades she directed the church choir.

It was exciting for the administrator-chaplain to go to Mrs. Leffingwell's home at 913 W. Main Street, Whitewater, and consummate the agreement signing. A lovely picture of her signing the agreement appeared in the Whitewater Register. This was another milestone, perhaps the word "breakthrough" could be used. "If Irene Leffingwell is doing this, surely others will follow." Indeed, others did follow. The floodgates were open and through the years many, many wonderful Whitewater area people have made their last earthly homes at Fairhaven. Many Whitewater area citizens and their relatives have also utilized the per diem services of the skilled nursing section.

Irene Leffingwell was completely convinced that her decision to reside at Fairhaven was a right one. She was asked to give a brief summary of her feelings at the Beloit Association meeting of the Wisconsin Congregational Conference, which was held at the Congregational Church, Whitewater. She spoke with feeling and clarity. Her physical appearance [white hair, smartly dressed, neat, clean, dignified] conveyed a message equal to her positive words about Fairhaven and her relationship to it.

The administrator-chaplain and Dentist O. J. Gates, a widower and a director of the Fairhaven board, from Fort Atkinson, Wisconsin, were sitting in a back pew when Irene spoke. Dr. Gates leaned over and said, "I'd really like to meet that woman. Can you introduce me?" After the meeting, the introduction was made. It blossomed into a courtship and ultimately those two wonderful persons were married. Instead of coming to live at Fairhaven immediately, Irene moved into the Gates residence in Fort Atkinson and the two shared marital happiness for quite a few years. After Dr. Gates died, Irene came to reside at Fairhaven in a type five apartment, just as she had planned years before. Her apartment was extremely attractive featuring Williamsburg blue carpeting, white curtains and drapery, and uplifting furniture, giving further evidence of what a first class person she was. It was truly a loss for Fairhaven when Irene suffered many minor strokes and finally returned to her Lord who had so richly blessed her life.

FIRST RESIDENTS: MARY S. BLACK AND JOSEPHINE FINNEY

The first residents to live at Fairhaven were Miss Mary S. Black, Fort Atkinson, Wisconsin, and Mrs. Josephine Finney, Luck [Amery], Wisconsin. Both arrived on November 15, 1962, and took up living in two apartments in Building E.

Extensive correspondence had flowed between Mrs. Finney and Fairhaven. The letters had covered in detail almost every aspect of projected Fairhaven life. Early on the morning of November 15th, the administrator-chaplain drove to Luck, Wisconsin, north of Amery, where Jo Finney was living in a nursing home. The car was loaded with Jo Finney's belongings, including several quality hybrid iris bulbs, which were later

Mary S. Black
Anderson Studio

Josephine Finney
Walt Peterson

planted on Fairhaven property and were enjoyed by the Fairhaven family for several years.

Upon arrival in Whitewater, late in the afternoon, an immediate walk through of Mrs. Finney's temporary apartment and the rest of Building E was made. With much surprise and delight it was discovered that Miss Mary Black had arrived and moved into an adjacent apartment unannounced, earlier in the day. How nice it was that there was immediate companionship. Administrator-chaplain and Marilyn Olm hosted both new residents for dinner at the parsonage. After dining and getting further acquainted, the residents returned to their apartments to spend a first night of residency.

Mary Black and Jo Finney were talented persons. Miss Black had taught school and was the principal of an elementary school in Nevada before her retirement and soon, thereafter, was honored when the school was named after her.

Josephine Finney was the widow of an electric company official. She assisted her husband in business capacities. Perhaps her greatest talent was that of oil painting. At over 80 years of age she oil painted a large picture of the Grand Teton mountains at Jennie Lake as a gift for Administrator-chaplain and Marilyn Olm. The picture is still prominently displayed in the Olm's home.

The following statement about the early days of residency at Fairhaven was written by Resident Finney and delivered by her November 15, 1967, on the occasion of Fairhaven's Fifth Anniversary Celebration of the arrival of residents:

> You know, the next time I apply for entrance to a retirement home, I'm going to make sure I'm not the first one to arrive, as this making of speeches just is not my cup of tea. However, I'm honored to be part of Fairhaven's Fifth Anniversary Celebration.
>
> The Fairhaven of today is a far cry from the Fairhaven of five years ago. It was a rather unique opening. Reverend Olm was the whole staff at that time and as he had driven 350 miles north to get me, there was no one here to receive Mary Black when she came that afternoon, earlier than expected. But, some of the workmen helped her get located. As Building E was the only one erected it wasn't a difficult job. Even E was not completely finished on the interior. There was no place to hang our clothes, and no window drapes, with workmen high on their trucks passing by from 7:00 A.M. on. We felt a bit uncomfortable about it, but I said, "If these men have never seen a grandma in her night

clothes, its just too bad!" Funny, neither Mary nor I are grand-mothers.

When Reverend Olm and I arrived at his home at 6:00 P.M., Mrs. Olm informed us of Mary's arrival. He went over and brought her back for a delicious dinner with us. The Olms were prepared to sleep us. Considering it an imposition, I asked Mary if she'd be afraid to sleep in Building E. She said, "No", so we hunted through our packing boxes for sheets, pillows, and blankets, and slept in Building E, all alone. The Olms invited us for breakfast but we declined as we were going shopping in the morning. So Mrs. Olm gave us some bread and butter. Mary had some coffee and we had a feast.

At 9:00 A.M. Miss [Ethel] Upham and Mrs. [Laura] Ferris of Whitewater came to take us shopping. From our entrance we had to walk over some wobbly boards laid on rocks to get to the road where a steady stream of bulldozers and tractors traveled. It was full of muddy pot holes and quite scary to get onto with the car. Once we got stuck, but they pulled us out.

I'd like to state here that we feel fortunate in being located in lovely Whitewater with its gracious people who looked after us in many ways. The city invited us to participate in its activities. Several of our Fairhavenites hold office in various organizations. We are grateful.

Reverend Olm came over cheerfully every morning to see how we were, and to clean the hall, etc. We cleaned our own apartments which were thick with dust every day for months. We had no matron or other help from November to January. For mechanical help and in emergencies, we asked the workmen. They were all gentlemen and very kind. I manned a telephone located in the storeroom, delivering messages to Reverend Olm and the construction crew located at the far end of Building C's basement a block away. To get there necessitated a walk partly in the open and over the floor of the basement which was heavily cluttered with debris which hid ends of pipes coming up through the floor. This called for some gingerly stepping for an old lady.

Now, the aforesaid is not intended as complaints. This is merely a statement of facts about the opening of Fairhaven which was having a hard time financially getting started; so it opened as soon as it could to bring in revenue. Never did I hear a complaint from any of them. We did what we could to help and sort of felt we were building our own home. We felt privileged to watch the development of Fairhaven. Nearly every day we walked through the buildings to see how they were progressing. Reverend Olm had a Herculean task. Credit must be given the Olm family also, who were on the job in every way. Bless them. Reverend Olm was a dedicated man if there ever was one, efficient in every phase of administration. His letters were so confidence-inspiring and satisfactory that I decided to tell him so. So I wrote saying, "Truly, Reverend Olm, you are the perfect administrator — so well chosen for Fairhaven." Apropos of this, I'm going to tell you a little story for which I'll probably be evicted: His immediate reply nearly toppled me from my chair: He wrote, "Did I ever feel my face turning red while reading the first paragraph of your letter. I feel I'm only doing my duty." [A revealing remark.] It warmed the heart. His reply showed he was humble, very human and had the common touch. It decided me to move to Fairhaven.

Reverend Olm also seems to have a sixth sense in choosing residents and heads of departments. I venture to say from chore boys up, including residents, we have as fine a class of persons as you can find in a community of this kind — all of which makes for a good rapport and a happy family. Free as birds; couldn't

Residents L-R: Jennie Schrage, Josephine Finney, and Mary Black with first auxiliary president Mary Henningsen at Tenth Anniversary of service to residents - 1972.

have better service; they really seem to care and aim to please — kindness prevails. It's like living at a club. People exclaim about the physical beauty of Fairhaven. I say you can't know the real beauty of Fairhaven until you have lived here. Again, apropos of that: One morning as I entered the main lounge on an errand, a man jumped at me from a group of visitors — "Do you work here?" he asked. "No-o-o, I live here," I told him. He came closer, half whispering, "Tell me, honestly, do you like it here?" "I love it," I said. With that a worldly looking lady jumped at him saying, "See! I *told* you so; they're all primed to say that." I was shocked but looked her straight in the face, saying, "Lady, we are *not primed* to say *anything!* What I said comes straight from the bottom of my heart! I mean it." I walked away. And that goes for today after having lived at Fairhaven for five years. You see I lived at another Home for six years, so I know what I'm talking about. Thanks for listening.

FIRST MINISTER COUPLE RESIDENTS

The Rev. and Mrs. Leo L. Duerson of Dousman, Wisconsin, were the first parish minister and wife to make firm application for residency. They entered the facility on August 1, 1963. Other ministers and missionaries came later, helping to fulfill one of the conference's goals, that being to provide retirement living for clergy and spouses.

THE "PIONEERS"

Early residents were called "the Pioneers." No one ever defined the cut-off point for being a pioneer — and it was interesting and amusing how many residents, who arrived much later, considered and described themselves as being pioneers.

The following residents arrived in sequence: [until August 15, 1964]

NAME	ENTRANCE DATE
Black, Mary	11-15-62
Finney, Josephine	11-15-62
Hitchcock, Jennie	11-17-62
Jenks, Jessie P.	11-14-62
Spradling, Genevieve	12-01-62
Robbins, M/M Leon H.	01-01-63
Saunders, Nellie	01-01-63

Merrihew, Ruth	01-08-63
Flohr, Hermine	01-24-63
Buske [Fogg], Edith	01-25-63
Walter, M/M C. H.	02-01-63
Makholm, Rose	03-01-63
Haworth, M/M William E.	03-28-63
Schrage, Jennie T.	04-01-63
Allen, Mary and Ruth	04-15-63
Koontz, Elsie	04-15-63
Graham, Mrs. Floyd	04-27-63
Sperry, Alice	04-30-63
Bell, Dorothy	05-01-63
Hitchcock, Mae	05-01-63
Prugger, May	05-08-63
Upham, Ethel	05-10-63
Rahr, Cora	05-24-63
Buske, Edward	06-13-63
Allyn, Margaret	06-14-63
Marshall, Mary	06-15-63
Haaker, M/M Herman	07-03-63
Nichols, M/M Edward	07-27-63
Duerson, Rev./M Leo L.	08-01-63
Marshall, Hazel	08-12-63
Burgess, M/M Lyle	08-29-63
DeLano, Bess	08-29-63
Hoffhine, M/M Charles	08-29-63
Liggett, M/M Thomas	08-29-63
Hoad, Rev. Alfred	09-01-63
Stine, Edna Y. 09-01-63	
Sauer, Verra	09-10-63
Bower, M/M Clarence	10-01-63
Comstock, Katherine	10-01-63
Weeks, Christine	10-10-63
Cnare, Faith	10-16-63

Krafft, Emma	10-18-63
Willett, Laura	10-26-63
Dexter, Dr. Emily	11-01-63
Swanson, Evelyn	11-03-63
Humphrey, M/M H.C.	11-11-63
Lauderdale, M/M Jesse	12-18-63
Maddock, M/M Horace	12-21-63
Arnold, M/M David	12-26-63
Hull, Florence	01-08-64
Leisk, Dorothy	01-15-64
Billings, Gertrude	02-15-64
Johnson, Rose A.	02-19-64
Boyd, Alice Ruth	02-26-64
Brewer, Fred J.	03-01-64
Meythaler, Lena	03-01-64
Schupp, M/M Carter	03-01-64
Brown, Clara E.	03-14-64
King, Mary L.	03-30-64
Shaw, Evelyn	04-29-64
Percy, Florence	05-30-64
Trebbe, Erna	05-02-64
Trieglaff, M/M Allen	05-09-64
Trippe, Klara	05-28-64
Hawley, M/M Clarence	06-16-64
Thompson, Hilda	06-30-64
Smith, Blake C.	06-30-64
Caldwell, Vera	07-01-64
Meyer, Elmer	07-08-64
Faulkner, M/M Russell	07-21-64
Tratt, Ruth	07-24-64
Bitzke, Flora V.	08-01-64
Cornell, William	08-01-64
Kirn, Edna	08-01-64
Austin, Helen M.	08-15-64
Hilbert, Ruby	08-15-64

Many "birds of the air" nested in the oak tree!

RESIDENT TESTIMONIES

Over the years, many residents have written comments on life at Fairhaven. These comments reflect personal feelings and the Fairhaven residential philosophy. Here are some of them:

Naomi Gander: I like Fairhaven for the warm friendliness of the residents, the staff and employees, the opportunities we have through programs to stretch our minds and our bodies and the pleasure of living in such pleasant surroundings.

Dorothy Bell, R. N.: I have lived at Fairhaven for over 22 years and I have always been glad I came.

Edith Knilans: I am thankful for Fairhaven. I love it here and can't think of any place I would rather be.

Herbert D. Bingham: When I first heard about Fairhaven I spelled it Fairheaven. I was not very wrong at that. When I came here to live, my first impression was the friendliness of those who live here and those who work here. Yes, Fairhaven could be called Fairheaven.

Professor Emeritus Warren Fisher: It's like home to me.

Alvira Winnie: Since making my home in Fairhaven thirteen years ago, I have enjoyed improved health, happiness and security. My only regret is that I did not come sooner.

Doris V. Higgins: I thank the Lord every day that I was led to Fairhaven, a church home, where independence, dignity, caring, fellowship and religion are so important.

Robert and Marie Hering: My husband and I are happy to be in Fairhaven. We like the friendly atmosphere and other residents. We like the cheerful employees, the security, the interesting programs and the many advantages of living here.

James F. Luther: I am pleased to have selected Fairhaven as my retirement home. Fairhaven offers just what I need, and I hope I have something to offer in return.

TRYING TO DEFINE THE "SPIRIT OF FAIRHAVEN"

The Board of Directors made an attempt to focus on the residential philosophy definition when in 1969 they requested the administrator-chaplain to express in words what was being called the "spirit of Fairhaven". Fifteen people were asked: "1] What is it that has made Fairhaven so unique? 2] Is there a philosophy or "spirit of Fairhaven" that can be expressed in words? 3] What ideals and ideas are behind and expressed in the policies, action and purpose at Fairhaven that seems so satisfying and needed by the residents?"

Residents, staff members and board members were asked to contribute. Selected contributions follow:

>*Resident Ruth Bennett:* As a resident of Fairhaven, thank you for the opportunity of writing this letter in an attempt to define "the spirit of Fairhaven" and also for the opportunity of expressing my own personal appreciation and thankfulness not only to all whose combined efforts made Fairhaven what it is but also for the privilege of making Fairhaven my home.

>For the past four years I have been a resident at Fairhaven, coming here immediately after I became eligible age-wise to enter. These have been very enjoyable years — not because I have spent them idly in the rocking chair, but because Fairhaven has contributed in so many ways to my well being and I hope, to some small degree, that I may have contributed to Fairhaven.

>Fairhaven is singular in itself as a Home for Senior Citizens. This uniqueness is reflected in many ways. The Christian atmosphere which prevails is outstanding. A family feeling and relationship is continually manifested by residents and staff by the spirit of helpfulness and good will . . . .

>The Fairhaven staff is of primary importance for the making of Christian living and "the Spirit of Fairhaven". Each in his or her own way, by tireless efforts, makes this Home outstanding. We are most fortunate in having an administrator-chaplain and a director of residential care, as well as all other staff members, dedicated to the promotion and fulfillment of the high standards of living which we, the residents, are privileged to enjoy. It would be impossible to adequately express in words the true worth of our staff.

>Fairhaven has an air of dignity not common to many senior citizen homes. The residents take real pride in their own personal grooming and are proud of the general appearance of the buildings and grounds . . . . .We are all very familiar with instances of elderly persons being subjected to undesirable and disagreeable domiciliary conditions and care during their latter years. Those of us here know the great asset, the infirmary, with its excellent staff, is to Fairhaven. For those of us without family to look after us but who have worked all of our lives and taken the responsibility of caring for our aged parents, the Fairhaven

infirmary lends an unexcelled feeling of security and that makes the infirmary a very integral part of the "Spirit of Fairhaven".

We who have lived in our comfortable and adequate apartments came here with an almost child-like trust in the Christian administration of Fairhaven. Fairhaven was intended to be a Christian family home for senior citizens with infirmary care when needed. . . . .

Better, perhaps, than I may define the "Spirit of Fairhaven" is found in Galatians 5:22-23 KJV: "But the fruit of the Spirit is love, joy, peace, long suffering, gentleness, goodness, faith, meekness, temperance; against such there is no law." How better than that may I define "the Spirit of Fairhaven"?

Head Resident William E. Markham, D.O.: Before retiring, Mrs. Markham and I visited several retirement homes with hopes of finding one to our liking, but found all of them lacking some things we desired. Then we heard about Fairhaven and came here. When we entered the front door, it just seemed to say, "Welcome!" We met Reverend Olm and were impressed even more. We were shown some apartments all with their own kitchens and complete baths, which the others did not have. Needless to say, we signed at once. We then waited until there was a vacancy. The day we moved in, everyone was very willing to help and made us feel at home because everyone leaves a house, friends and memories of many years to come here.

The administrator-chaplain's office is always open and you are always welcome if you have a problem or just want to visit. Whatever your faith you can feel free to talk to Reverend Olm.

The infirmary with its efficient nurses and aides is the Angel of Mercy — always a smile and tender care. It seems to me Fairhaven means, "We care about you."

Board Member Don Faulkner: The spiritual and temporal have been combined in the direction of Fairhaven with the spiritual being dominant. I believe that this combination used with excellent Christian leadership has resulted in a humanness and is expressed in "tender loving care" of each resident. This approach has kept Fairhaven from becoming "institutionalized", austere or businesslike.

The ideals are those expressed in the Christian religion, especially "love one another." This concept has been carried through into the policies that the administrator has used in the

daily management of Fairhaven. The result has been to provide
the last home on this earth in which the resident receives not
only superior creature comfort but spiritual refreshment.

However it has been accomplished, the residents seem to
have a real zest for life, a creativity in the projects that keep them
busy and a happy view on life.

Former Board Member Clarence Peck: In response to your
request for a statement of opinion concerning the "spirit of
Fairhaven," may I remind you that once I asked you to define for
me the term "Holy Spirit?" I believe the things I've seen happen
at Fairhaven have given me a better conception of that term.

Fairhaven as we see it today as an instrument of our church,
is the result of the concepts of Christian service on the part of
many people, clergy and laity alike, which converged, after being
tested in the rapids of adversity, and have since been blessed by
the hand of the Almighty to become a true "fair haven" for the
elderly who have need for a sense of security in their declining
years.

Thus I believe the "spirit of Fairhaven" is unique in that it is
the sum total of the individual concepts of the "Holy Spirit" as
held by all of the individuals who planned it and those who later
were given the opportunity to operate it.

As you found difficulty in defining the term "Holy Spirit", so
do I find difficulty in expressing, in words, my concept of the
"spirit of Fairhaven". It's probably different in meaning to each
person involved.

Staff Member Dorothy Fuller: What makes Fairhaven so
unique, to me, is the wonderful Christian atmosphere which prevails in our Home. [I sensed it the very first time I walked
through the corridors.] There is an air of warm friendliness,
brotherly love, and Christian fellowship. One can see it on the
faces of the residents. I am certain as I talk with them daily, that
they have the feeling of serenity and security — two very important factors to one growing older.

Christian ideals are expressed in the purpose of Fairhaven.
Respect for everyone — be one resident or staff — is exemplified
in the policy. The friendly greetings exchanged by everyone; the
privilege of living one's own life and yet being a part of the
Family when one cares to; and the knowledge that you will
receive immediate care when ill, is a fine example of action.

These three goals could not be reached were it not for the fine leadership and encouragement you give. Many times I find myself humming as I work because "my cup is so full". I thank God daily for the opportunity of being a part of Fairhaven. It is a joy to me.

Former Staff Member Alida Kneisel, R. N.: I have tried to focus on what to me are the intangible qualities that are more general, but which contribute to the essence of the climate of Fairhaven, regardless of transitory changes. Naturally, my comments are influenced by my nurse perspective.

To me, the overall philosophy of Fairhaven is that it is dedicated to nurturing and sustaining a dynamic environment in which that spark of divinity that is within each and everyone may continue to glow and grow toward its ultimate destiny with God.

Some of the ideas and ideals that I think are inherent in this philosophy are: 1. There is respect for and an appreciation of the dignity and worth of each individual. 2. There is a recognition of the fact that as mobility declines and as infirmities encroach upon the independence of the aging individual, the staff can gradually assume responsibility for augmenting the needs of the individual, without detracting from that dignity. That is to say, that the programs and policies of Fairhaven are so structured that the residents' needs can be met in ways that allow them to exercise their independence to the maximum of their potential as long as possible. Yet the policies are flexible enough to provide basic needs as the resident's role gradually shifts from one of independence to dependency.

There are some specifics that I think play an important part in Fairhaven's uniqueness:

1. Because of its location and layout, the residents can remain in intimate contact with nature and thereby retain a sense of oneness with the universe.

2. It is a community of individuals that is not isolated from the larger community, but rather is an integral and positive force within the town in which it is situated. . . . .

3. Because of the physical plan and organization of Fairhaven, there arises a sense of neighborhood within the various structural entities. Between the residents in each of these units there is generated an aura of mutually supportive relationships and loyalties such as exist in a family. In times of personal stress and loneliness, there is a sensitivity between individuals of

a unit that reaches out and sustains the individual who is in need
of comfort and loving concern. . . .

Administrator-chaplain Carroll J. Olm: Jesus said, "The
Kingdom of God [comes] not with observation; neither shall they
say, Lo here! or, lo there! For behold, the Kingdom of God is
within you!" [Luke 17:20,21 KJV.] The Kingdom of God is within
you! Here is God at work in the world. God chooses to work
through people chosen for peculiar tasks. People opening their
hearts for the accomplishment of God's will. In Proverbs we
read, "As [a man thinks] in his heart, so is he." [Proverbs 23:7
KJV.] We make ourselves what we are by our faiths, our hopes,
our loves and our thoughts.

Some have equated this with the Spirit of God or the Holy
Spirit. When one's heart is touched by the Spirit of God, then that
person maintains integrity, has a sense of community, knows and
accepts responsibilities to God and to others, loves God and
neighbor. The tenets of the Christian faith, life and community
are expressed. The words of Paul in Galations 6:2, "You obey the
law of Christ when you offer each other a helping hand," become
real.

Fairhaven's motto "Where Life Is Added To Years" reflects
the statement in the prologue used by John: "In Him was life!"
[John 1:4 KJV.] That is, in Christ is life. Where do you see people
walking about with a light in their eyes and smiles on their faces?
"[Those] who [have] the Son [have] life!" [I John 5:12 KJV.] There
is where you find it. The Christian religion gives new purpose,
new zest for living. No wonder bodies, if they get sick, get sick in
a different way and respond both to medicine and prayer in a different way. No wonder they rise above trouble and disappoint-
ment. No wonder you see in them a kind of joy and radiance that
you find nowhere else. The days in the flesh take on new dimensions for *He* gives "life and that abundant!"

The Spirit of God "within" will effectuate service and love in
as many ways as there are people who will be willing to be the
vehicles of that Spirit, but when all these expressions are inter-
relating one to another, then we sense the unique in the life of
Christian community.

The Fairhaven spirit, or the Spirit of God, is difficult to
define since it is not only invisible but also is without structure
and has no specific formula. It is relative to the extent that it can

be sporadic, spontaneous, voluminous according to the degree the Spirit controls. Yet it is in every sense real and productive.

The personalities of board members, the administrator-chaplain, other employees, residents, volunteers and even visitors are important and do contribute to the warmth and success of Fairhaven. However, the spirit of Fairhaven is bigger than any one or even several personalities.

The spirit of Fairhaven is the sum total of God's Spirit in all lives involved in the Fairhaven ministry. Thus Fairhaven is God's and the spirit of Fairhaven is the Spirit of God.

RESIDENT AGREEMENTS
AND THE ADMISSIONS COMMITTEE

Two areas of Christian labor — the progression of residency agreements and the work of the Admissions Committee — had significant effect on the residency. Countless hours were devoted to each of these arenas of service. The decisions made had lasting positive effect on those who came to live at Fairhaven.

The Progression of Resident Agreements

A considerable number of persons were willing to commit to future residency at Fairhaven, but they were not ready to begin residency immediately after construction was to be completed and apartments were to become available. Hence, even before the first residents arrived, a waiting list developed.

The Deferred Residency Agreement

To accommodate these future residents, a contract called the Deferred Residency Agreement was written and implemented. This agreement, signed by the future residents and the administrator-chaplain, became effective after an application fee of $500 was received by the corporation. [Later this fee was increased to $750.]

Applicants were permitted to sign Deferred Residency Agreements before the residency eligibility age of 65 years, as long as they were at least 55 years of age.

The application fee [which applied on the resident's founders fee upon admission] was charged to assure a bonafide waiting list. It was made sufficiently high to "weed out" curiosity seekers and others who were not really earnest about future residency, but not so high that it would be exorbitant.

The signer of the Deferred Residency Agreement derived benefits, such as:

[1] Opportunity to be on the waiting list with expectation of having residency offered in an apartment of one or more of the types selected by the signer and set forth in his/her agreement.

[2] Counseling services of Fairhaven as the person looked toward residency.

[3] Priority over others for admission to Fairhaven's "Residency Plus" level of service. By being on the waiting list, the person received opportunity to enter this level of care before others. This supportive service included all housekeeping, all food service, laundry and bed making, administration of medication, night checks, emergency call system, supervision, occupational therapy, physical therapy, etc. Nursing service was available in the skilled nursing section.

[4] Many hours of time and service went into the making of an application. The processing of an application exacted many staff hours with the person, first as a visitor, then as an interested party, subsequently as an applicant, and finally as a member on the waiting list.

Fairhaven is one of those very few homes where a person who made application for deferred residency could be on the waiting list, be offered an apartment and retain his/her position on the waiting list without dropping to the bottom of the list. It was not unusual, when an apartment became available, that ten or more waiting list names would be passed over [people continued to defer entrance] before the contacted person would be ready and willing to become a resident.

One significant reason for Fairhaven's development was to provide a facility for Congregationalists. Never was it to be designated as exclusively for Congregational members. The doors were to be open for people of all faiths — and those who professed no faith.

The Board of Directors grappled with the residency priority for Congregationalists issue. Board members were aware that the conference constituency wanted a place for conference local church members to spend their retirement years. The directors were also aware that these same Congregationalists had generously supported [and continue to support] the Fairhaven ministry with financial contributions. Without that support, Fairhaven would never have achieved building completion. Within two years after the birth of the Wisconsin Conference of the United Church of Christ, the members of the new United Church of

Christ in Wisconsin had demonstrated liberal financial support for Fairhaven. [That support continues through the United Conference Appeal of the Wisconsin Conference of the United Church of Christ.]

It was never a question whether or not Congregationalists [United Church of Christ members] should receive some residency priority. The question was what kind of priority should it be.

After thorough and prayerful discussion, policy was enacted providing for the creation of two waiting lists:

[1] List A to be composed of all Congregational [United Church of Christ] members. A member to be defined as: Any person who was a member of a Congregational [United Church of Christ] church for five of the last 20 years. This definition developed after some persons transferred church membership to gain better priority for admission. [Not in all cases would this assumption have proven beneficial, for in some years, and for some apartments, List A [Congregational-United Church of Christ] was more than three times as long as List B [non-Congregational-United Church of Christ].

[2] List B to be composed of all those who were not Congregational [United Church of Christ] members.

The policy stated that for each type apartment, persons from List A were to be admitted three times and then one person [persons in case of a couple] was [were] to be admitted from List B. If and when an apartment was available for resident admission and all persons on List A were contacted, resulting in no one wanting to be admitted, those on List B were to be contacted. Such an admission from List B would still count as a List A priority usage.

The Immediate Residency Agreement

At the time a deferred resident became an actual resident, another agreement, called the Immediate Residency Agreement, was signed. The Immediate Residency Agreement superseded the Deferred Residency Agreement, guaranteed services, and granted the resident leasing rights to a specific apartment, selected by the resident.

The Deferred Residency Agreements and the Immediate Residency Agreements were amended many times over the first decades for improvement, for clarification, to cover issues and situations which only became evident after some years of experience, and to include clauses which covered new areas of residency life and governing, not previously entertained or anticipated. The agreements were adjusted and improved from time to time to meet the challenges of changing times.

Fairhaven "lived up" to its agreements. If changes to residency agreements were made adversely affecting the benefits residents received, the earlier clauses in previously executed residency agreements were honored, unless the resident agreed to the adverse changes and signed a new agreement validating the same.

In the first three decades, there was only one agreement change that adversely affected the residents in a significant way. When the original agreements were written and implemented, our nation had not as yet experienced run-away inflation. The conference leaders and the members of the Fairhaven Board of Directors wanted to guarantee residents that Fairhaven would never take advantage of them financially after they made Fairhaven their home. Hence, a clause guaranteeing that monthly rates would never increase more than 5% per year, was included in the early agreements. The nation experienced significant inflation in the late 1960's. Annual double-digit inflation almost became common in the 1970's. It became obvious that the corporation could no longer sustain itself operationally without addressing the 5% limitation clause. The dilemma was explained to residents and all but five residents signed codicils to their agreements that deleted the 5% limitation clause. The five residents who did not sign such a codicil decided to keep their residency agreement intact. They paid monthly rates as protected by the 5% limitation clause. Voluntary donations were made to the corporation to cover the difference between their rates and the new rates that the rest of the residency was paying. There was concern, but no controversy.

Agreements signed prior to 1966 contained inadequate definition as to physician and infirmary care [skilled nursing] benefits for residents. Clarification was made by giving all life lease residents a daily discount on skilled nursing rates. Later agreements were adjusted when the corporation became an approved Medicare facility.

An agreement change was enacted for applicants of Type 6 apartments that limited these apartments to married couples, with surviving spouse agreeing to move to a single apartment. Rationale for this change was based on Fairhaven rapidly becoming devoid of married couples. Freeing up Type 6 apartments [18 in number] for married couples enhanced the total residency life by increasing thereby the number of male residents. Later, when expansions provided additional "double" apartments, thereby automatically increasing greater opportunities for married couple admission, the restriction on Type 6 apartments was rescinded with proper change in the agreements.

In 1972, the resident adjustment period was changed from a 90 day period after admission to a 30 day period after admission. During the adjustment period, the resident could terminate residency, for any reason, without financial penalty. During the period of adjustment, the corporation could also exercise rights to terminate the residency agreement, for any reason. After ten years of experience, staff had recommended the change. Whether or not the resident would prove to be a suitable resident could be satisfactorily determined within 30 days. The reduction of the adjustment period from 90 days to 30 days reduced by 60 days the insecurity some residents experienced during the adjustment period. It also reduced the exposure the corporation had to refund all application fee and founders fee payments, without penalty of any kind, should a resident terminate residency.

Ten years later, an agreement change protected the corporation against any resident decision to divest all personal assets and then lean to the corporation for financial support for the rest of his or her life. Never did the corporation ever discharge a resident for the resident lacking financial resources. However, divestment by a resident rested outside the spirit of the agreements. Applicants understood and accepted this amendment without protest.

Over the years, changes were also made in the Deferred Residency Agreements. After five years of operation, the agreements specifically stated that the application fee was not refundable in the event the applicant died before becoming a resident. Rationale for this position is cited on page 114.

In 1971, a clause was added to the agreement assuring the applicant that the application fee could continue to be applied on the founders fee, if the applicant was offered an apartment, but continued to defer residency.

From time to time the board of directors increased the amounts of founders fees for new residents. The agreements were amended to reflect the possibility of any changes in the application fee or the founders fee.

Reviewing and upgrading of agreements was a continuous process. The Board of Directors wanted the agreements to be the best possible to protect the rights of both the residents and the corporation. Whenever the agreements were updated, full consideration to the residents was always given. Challenges to the agreements were almost non-existent during the first three decades.

The Board of Directors and administration depended, for legal matters, almost entirely on the ability, judgment and wisdom of Attorney and Board Member William J. Willis. His guiding hand was upon every document involving resident agreements for the first three decades [and continued well into the fourth decade.]

Fairhaven was protected from possibility of lawsuits because Attorney Willis' legal advice and professional workmanship helped to create resident agreements that were readable, forthright, easy to understand, and fair to all parties involved.

Resident agreements were printed double-spaced and in large print. The administrator-chaplain read aloud the agreements with applicants before signatures were attached.

The Admissions Committee

Persons interested in becoming residents of Fairhaven read materials describing the program, visited the facility, usually on several occasions, had conversations with tour guides, residents and staff members, and were oriented by the administrator-chaplain.

After an application for residency was completed, all materials were shared with the admissions committee. Committee members reviewed the application and then made the decision to accept or reject the applicant[s] for future residency.

Admissions committee members were appointed by the board of directors, with the administrator-chaplain ex officio. Almost always, the meetings of the committee were held in the home of a committee member. Frequently, the meeting duration was three hours or more. For three decades, coffee was always available.

The very first committee was composed of Nellie Saunders, Whitewater, and the Rev. Donald S. Hobbs, pastor of Congregational Church [now Congregational Church United Church of Christ,] Whitewater, and the administrator-chaplain. Most members were residents of the City of Whitewater and all were members of the Congregational Church [now United Church of Christ.] Over the first three decades, the following persons served:

> Nellie Saunders
> The Rev. Donald S. Hobbs
> Thelma Rockwell
> Virginia Theune
> The Rev. Phillip Day
> The Rev. Dary Hennemann
> The Rev. Trent Rockwell, Burlington, Wisconsin
> Elizabeth Kincaid, Palmyra, Wisconsin
> H. Jane Morphew
> Mary Dalee
> The Rev. Carroll J. Olm, ex officio.

Each meeting opened with prayer for Divine guidance. All aspects of an applicant's life were reviewed: biographical, education, job history, activities, likes and dislikes, church membership, financial status and at least three personal references. If necessary, additional references were pursued. In one case, over 15 personal references were obtained before the committee felt it had received sufficient information to make a proper and fair decision.

Not all applicants were approved.

Two admissions committee members have given special longevity service. Thelma Rockwell, chairperson, and Virginia Theune, secretary, after serving for over 25 years, were given the Honor Award for Meritorious Service. [September 10, 1989.] At the time of this writing [1997], Thelma Rockwell continues as committee chair. She is now in her 30th year of chairing the committee. That longevity record may well stand for a long time, if not forever. Thanks and praise be to God for such dedication and service.

When the honors were conferred, there were two unique aspects experienced:

Thelma Rockwell - 1989
Lauri Ahlman

Virginia Theune - 1989
Helgesen

[1] It was the first time that the award was given to two individuals simultaneously.

[2] It was the only time that both a husband and a wife had
received the award. Dr. Warren S. Theune, Janesville [formerly
Whitewater], had previously been awarded the honor in 1979 for
his service on the Fairhaven Board of Directors. He had represented the Fairhaven ministry in the Whitewater community with
distinction and in special dimensions.

Virginia Theune shared the following reflections of her years on the
committee:

Fairhaven attracted fine people. This made the admissions
committee's work easier. After reading the applicant's creden-
tials and references, we were anxious for the applicants to come
and make their home in Fairhaven. The majority of applicants
had served their communities and churches well. The strength of
Fairhaven will always come from its residents.

Having served on the admissions committee for 25 years, I
was able to meet and become acquainted with many of the residents that we had processed. It was a joy to know how Fairhaven
had met a need in their lives and realize how happy they were
that they had decided to leave their home towns and come to
Fairhaven in Whitewater.

I saw Fairhaven grow in many ways; not only in its physical
buildings, but in service to residents and its outreach to the
whole Whitewater community.

It was always enjoyable to work for Fairhaven by serving on
the admissions committee.

The oak tree became a haven for God's loved ones!

CHAPTER IX

Oldster Funny Bones

". . .A. . .sense of humor. . .is the next best thing
*to an abiding faith in providence." *1*
G.B. Cheever

Long faces and austere lives might have been the norm for stoics and separatists, but such did not find a place in life at Fairhaven. Residents were not immune from physical suffering and many of the other anxieties or stresses of life. However, residents understood the goal. They tried to live above the distresses to find the cloud's silver lining, to minimize the negatives, to find the good, the beautiful, and the humorous in every situation. Surely, the Lord desires that followers of Christ should be happy and enjoy the whole pale of Divine creation.

Good humor is consistent with living a dignified life. Humor brings "spice" to relationships. It creates atmosphere to produce smiles and relaxation.

After visiting Fairhaven, Doris Ann Krupinski wrote, "Wandering the corridors of a retirement home, one gets a sense of what tickles the funny bone at an advanced age." *2 Add to that how unintentional slips, loss of memory, can produce unintended ticklers.

During the three decades, there were many ticklers, not only initiated by residents, but in given cases, by employees or others. A few examples follow:

. . . . . A wheelchair resident was ready to pay the Beautician Gerry Wilcox for her shampoo and set. She retrieved her purse from below her wheelchair pad, whereupon the beautician said, "You know, you're the only person I know who sits on her assets."

. . . . . At the celebration of their 60th wedding anniversary, Resident Clarence Bower, the male spouse, was flirting with a young nurse. His resident friend, Retired Professor William

*1 Reprinted from *Useful Quotations* published 1934.
*2 February 1988 - View From the Hill - *"A Dose of Reality Can Be Too Dangerous."*

Cornell, asked him, "Don't you think your wife will be jealous when you do things like that?"

"I surmise she will," he answered, "but I don't want her ever to think that she has a sure thing."

. . . . . A totally visually handicapped resident, Eleanor Stein, was drinking coffee with several other women residents in the main lounge. They saw a male resident walking by in the company of another female resident. The women began to "chit-chat" about what they saw.

"Are they going together?" one asked.

"Why certainly!" replied her friend.

"Why, I didn't know that," responded the former.

"Yes, that's been going on for some time."

"Well, what do you know about that? I didn't realize. . . . ."

After hearing what her friends said, the "blind" resident commented, "For goodness sake, you'd have to be stone blind not to be able to see that." Eleanor, after realizing what she had said, laughed louder than the others.

. . . . . A retired University of Wisconsin - Whitewater professor came to Fairhaven one day and shared, "Every married couple passes through three stages of argumentation:

The first one-third of their married life they argue about money.

The second one-third they argue about their children.

During the last one-third they argue about when to take their milk of magnesia.

Sometimes the humorous carries significant meaning and sensitivity:

. . . . . A 90 plus year old minister, the Rev. Arthur Brown, who served his Lord and the church for 60 years, visited his ill wife in the skilled nursing section several times a day for over three years.

Upon the death of his wife he continued to come to the skilled nursing floor to seek out his wife. The patterns were deeply entrenched.

The second time he came, the director of nursing confronted him saying, "Reverend, are you here looking for your wife?"

"Yes!" he replied.

"Reverend, your wife died and we buried her. You know that!"

There was a long pause, whereupon the Reverend said, "Yes, I know that, but you'll have to help me to remember it."

. . . . . The same Reverend Arthur Brown taught a Bible study class at Fairhaven. At the end of one study session he summarized what he had tried to project to the members of his class, using the words of the hymn *Be Strong, We Are Not Here To Play*. The Reverend said emphatically, "WE ARE NOT HERE TO PLAY!"

Whereupon, Resident Jennie Schrage elbowed visitor Virginia Theune and whispered, "Too, bad! I play all the time."

. . . . . Ninety year old Betsy Holbrook was getting ready to accompany her son to the Duck Inn restaurant for Sunday dinner. Unfortunately, she fell and fractured her collarbone.

While she was waiting to go to the hospital, the attending Registered Nurse Ellen Wiedenhoeft, overheard her say to another resident, "I was going to Duck Inn, but I guess I'll have to "duck out."

The following appeared in the Whitewater Register:

. . . . . A foreign student from University of Wisconsin - Whitewater was chatting the other day with a man from Fairhaven, the local home for senior citizens. The subject: marriage. The student wanted to know something about making a marriage work.

"Well," said the man, "When you're single, you're incomplete. When you're married, you're finished."

. . . . . In 1984, one of our maiden residents went to the doctor's office for examination.

"You know, doctor," she said, "you're the first man in 90 years to ask me to pull my pants down."

. . . . . Social service employees had been urging all residents to have their living wills executed.

A vivacious resident burst into their office and forthrightly said, "I want one of those forms that says you can die any time you want to."

. . . . . Administrator-chaplain Olm and his wife, Marilyn, were in the Milwaukee airport at Concourse B. After passing through security detection control, Mrs. Olm needed to use the women's room.

"Use the one right here." Dr. Olm said, "I'll wait for you and then we can go to the gate."

Upon returning, Marilyn asked, "What was that loud roar of laughter I heard?"

"You should have been here. A dignified 90 plus year old man, in a wheelchair, wearing a black suit, white shirt and tie, approached the security area, but couldn't walk through the detection unit. An attractive woman security guard courteously explained that she was required to wave a magnetic hand detector over him — and she did. After replacing the detector, she confronted him and politely asked, "Do you mind if I touch you now?"

There was a long, silent pause.

After thinking about it, the man looked up at her and sweetly replied, "Depends on how far you want to go."

. . . . . Long-time Whitewater resident Heywood Humphrey resided in skilled nursing. He had difficulty remembering and, typically, got things confused.

One day the administrator-chaplain entered his room and said, "Good morning, Heywood Humphrey, and isn't it a nice day?"

Heywood responded in a gruff voice, "Who are you?"

"I'm the Rev. Carroll Olm."

Again gruffly, "What are you doing here?"

"Well, I'm the administrator-chaplain of Fairhaven."

Heywood said, "I don't know you."

"Oh, yes you do, Heywood Humphrey. You and I have known each other for over ten years. We met in your Century Office Supply store on Center Street, downtown Whitewater."

"Humph! You sure didn't make much of an impression."

. . . . . Resident Loretta Norenberg, widow of Jess Norenberg, reported she observed two hard of hearing residents chatting in the lounge.

One said, "Laura Ferris is 100 years old today."

"Yes, I heard that, too. I think she's in the infirmary."

"I wonder if she is senile."

"Oh, I don't think so, I'm pretty sure she's Congregational."

. . . . . In 1970, after the Olm family returned from a European trip, residents enjoyed hearing about everything that happened, especially this aftermath story which produced lots of giggles:

Fifteen year old Beth Ann was on the family room floor, surrounded by several of her closest friends. She talked about her trip experience saying, " Girls, I can go all over Europe and get along just fine by using only five German words."

"Really, Beth, what are those words?" the girls asked.

"These five," Beth said, "Wo ist Die Toilette, bitte?" [Where is the toilet, please?]

. . . . . Gregg Theune, reared in Whitewater and a student at University of Wisconsin - Whitewater, was employed part-time in the maintenance department. He worked irregular hours on no particular daily schedule. One late afternoon a resident approached him and said, "I haven't seen you around here. Are you new here?"

Gregg answered, "No, I've been working here for some time."

"Well, what is your name?"

"My name is Gregg."

"Say that again, please," the resident said.

Gregg said louder, "My name is *Gregg*!"

"Young man, speak up — louder — I'm an old lady and I'm hard of hearing."

Somewhat disgruntled, Gregg spoke very loudly, "***My name is Gregg!***" And then he spelled it out loudly and distinctly, "***G - R - E - G - G — GREGG***!"

With a smile the dear woman responded, "Oh, thank you, Rex!"

. . . . . In 1985, Resident Helen M. Huling wrote a letter to the Olm family as follows:

Reading of Rev. Olm's projected trip to Israel/Egypt, I figure he may see a mummy.

Years ago John and I took a small grandson with us when we visited a museum, where we looked at a mummy. Our little grandson pulled himself up to peek into the casket, looked up at us and said, "That's not a Mommy. That's a Daddy!"

. . . . . Dietitian and Food Service Supervisor Constance Hornickel noticed Resident Hazel Hessing was eating only a part of her dinner. Connie approached her saying, "Should I cut up your liver for you?"

Quick as a wink, Miss Hessing said, "No thank you. That's the only one I've got."

. . . . . In 1981, 93 year old Nellie Newell was asked, "Is there something we can do for you?"

Without hesitation, Nellie blurted out, "Yes, I need a man."

. . . . . In October 1987, Resident University of Wisconsin - Whitewater Professor Emeritus Warren Fisher was wearing spotted ties. Twenty of his ties were cleaned by staff and laid out for his use.

The next day the director of nursing approached him saying, "Why are you wearing that dirty tie? Put on one of the clean ones!"

He replied, "But they're all clean and I want to keep them that way."

. . . . . Five years before, the same Resident Fisher was downtown Whitewater and met a former colleague whom he hadn't seen for 20 years.

"Well, Warren, what do you think about this business of getting old?"

Professor Fisher responded, "It's the 'damnedest' thing that's ever happened to me in my life."

. . . . . Humor even creeps into letters from former employees. Law student and former employee Steven Sents was seeking some part time work. On November 5, 1981, he wrote, "I am writing to inquire whether you might have any need for extra help over Christmas time. . . . . Law school is definitely a challenging experience for me. I do not think I have felt this dumb since I put the tractor in the creek."

. . . . . During the construction of the addition to Building C and the second floor of Building D, Residents Mae Kachel and Dorothy Klatt were watching excavation efforts from the glassed in C-D walkway. They were sidewalk superintendents super plus.

A gentleman came and stood next to the residents. For some time he observed the workers in action, but said nothing.

Finally, Mae Kachel approached him saying, "Do you have any questions about the building going on here? We live here and we'd be happy to tell you all about what they are doing."

"Oh, that won't be necessary," the visitor said. "You see, I'm the architect."

. . . . . On November 10, 1981, a new nursing assistant, after her second day of employment, was reporting a matter resting heavy on her mind to the director of nursing. "I don't want to cause trouble and I am not wanting to talk about anyone, but it seems to me that Claudine Henry [ward clerk] has an affair going with that man, Frank, from maintenance [maintenance supervisor].

Laughingly, the director reassured her, "Don't be concerned. Next week Claudine and Frank will be celebrating their 39th wedding anniversary."

. . . . . An 85 year old skilled nursing resident was regularly receiving the medication RIOPAN.

Using her walker, she approached the central nursing station and addressed the R.N.'s and L.P.N.'s, who were in an evaluation session. "Tomorrow Henry H. is coming to pick me up and I want to know how I can carry my DIAPHRAIM."

The staff roared!

The resident giggled saying, "Oh, I didn't mean that."

. . . . . Jim Olm worked part time in maintenance. One of his daily duties was to push the large dust mop over the asphalt tile in the quarter of a mile corridors [before they all were carpeted.]

One evening, Jim came home and said, "You know, residents often have their doors open when I'm pushing the mop through the corridors — and you know, for that whole quarter of a mile and back, I never miss a beat of the Lawrence Welk show."

. . . . . Resident Julia Berg, *at 98 years of age*, was transported in a wheelchair from her apartment to the well equipped, large bath room on the skilled nursing floor so she could have her attended periodic bath.

As she was wheeled off the elevator on to the floor, *a 70 plus year old*, ambulatory resident passed her when entering the elevator.

After the elevator doors closed, Resident Berg looked up at the nursing assistant and asked, "Who is that old woman that just passed us?"

[Only "other people" get old!]

. . . . . Resident Hulda J. P. Olm, mother of the administrator-chaplain, was accompanying her son, her daughter-in-law, Marilyn, and her two grandsons, Mark and Jim, to the Madison Coliseum to see the performance of the Vienna Lipizan horses.

Grandma Olm said, "You know, there's one thing I don't understand about Fairhaven residents."

"What's that?" her son asked.

"Well, we know that some of the women smoke, but they only smoke in their apartments behind closed doors. Why don't they just come out and smoke in the open?"

No one responded. There was silence for what seemed a minute.

Finally, Grandson Mark softly spoke, "Well, grandma, maybe they do that for the same reason you ask Jimmy and me to come over to get your empty pony beer bottles and dispose of them in the parsonage trash container."

Grandma laughed the loudest!

. . . . . One of the very precious humorous episodes came from a youngster of First United Methodist Church of Whitewater.

Mrs. Kathy Johnson brought her Sunday School class to Fairhaven on a Sunday morning. The class of first graders toured part of the facility, talked with residents and then ended their visit with discussion and worship in Fairhaven's fellowship hall.

Upon returning to his mother, one little boy was asked, "What did you do today?"

"Mom, I've been somewhere." he said.

Mother, probing more, added: "And did you see lots of old people there?"

"Oh no,mom," the little boy replied, "All we saw was lots of grandpas and grandmas!"

PRAISE BE TO GOD!

CHAPTER X

The Staff

"God likes help when helping people."
Irish Proverb

In earlier chapters, focus was given to how theology, philosophy, concepts and administration contributed to the quality and uniqueness of the Fairhaven ministry. Then, the contributions generated from the character, personalities, commitment and attitudes of the residency were lifted up. Another contributor, the Fairhaven staff, spanned the first two. Staff interpreted and carried out policies. Staff translated ideas and words into realities. Staff provided the "hands on" service.

Proper selection, orientation and education of employees were vitally needed if Fairhaven were to achieve its goals.

Many times the question was asked, "How do you hire such excellent employees?" A local businessman came to the administrator-chaplain's office to seek information as to how Fairhaven selected and trained employees. He had observed the success Fairhaven experienced and wanted to incorporate Fairhaven methods into his business. He said, "In several instances Fairhaven hired persons, who were less than satisfactory in other jobs, but who 'blossomed' into excellent productive employees at Fairhaven. What do you do? How do you do it? We want to practice the same procedures, if you tell us how it's done."

There was no mystery or secret in how Fairhaven did it. Specific intentional methods, policies, standards, ideas were pursued. Fairhaven administrative staff never felt the possession of any magical touch in the selection of employees. Without doubt, most of the traditional techniques of employee recruitment were applied. We sought persons who were qualified and experienced. We looked for pleasant personalities, intelligence, experience, religious commitment, a spirit of cooperation, control of temper, a loving heart, neatness, and ability to communicate.

Every adaptable idea to enhance the process of getting and orienting and training good employees was thoroughly considered. That Fairhaven attracted and engaged and maintained good employees is a fact. Was it 100% so? No! The great, great majority of department heads and departmental employees, who worked under the department heads, were assets to the program. They not only absorbed, but helped to implement the

Christian religious concept and philosophy upon which Fairhaven was founded and under which Fairhaven was operated.

Many employees — beginning with the administrator-chaplain — testified and testify that God led them to serve through the Fairhaven ministry. There were instances when such feelings of Divine guidance were felt in advance of being hired for work at Fairhaven. Such feelings might have surfaced after the employee experienced what it was like to work in an altruistic setting. Nevertheless, that God had a significant part in leading specific people to work at Fairhaven in specific capacities is not denied by the believers who lived the experience.

A considerable number of excellent employees applied for Fairhaven positions because of their friends or relatives. Those who were employed at Fairhaven, recommended that Fairhaven was a quality workplace where all persons were treated fairly, as equals. They experienced a pleasant environment, where genuine appreciation was expressed for every employee's service. Compensation, with benefits, was more than satisfactory. One quality employee attracts another quality employee. The adage "Birds of a feather, flock together," applied.

While there may be no hard data to support the idea, it seems that not-for-profit, church-related, Christian motivated causes do attract people who are altruistic and benevolent minded — people who have a tender heart.

Applicants believe they can serve God and humankind more easily in that type setting. They want to enjoy the compensations [the inner satisfactions] which come when one's work, with hands-on touch, directly enhances the status of the person served. Thus, the job is more than a job; it's a mission. It's helping to "bear one another's burden." It's seeing Christ in the least of humanity.

Employees were reminded in orientation and training sessions that working at Fairhaven embraced more than just earning dollars and cents. Employees were told that if the only reason they were working at Fairhaven was the pay check, that administration would prefer they would seek employment elsewhere. Motivation for work at Fairhaven should be the act of service — "giving the cup of cold water"— helping to alleviate the fears, the pain, the suffering, the sorrow, the frustrations, the confusions, the insecurities, and/or the anxieties of the elderly being served. Yes, everyone needs and wants a paycheck, but that should not be why employees worked at Fairhaven. The job compensation goes far beyond the selfish aspect of employment.

When the corporation is Christian, not-for-profit, the emphasis is not rigidly focused on the "bottom line." To balance the budget, to make ends meet, to be good managers, to be good stewards, to keep resident rates as low as possible, were the goals pursued. Doing what was fair — what was right — was as important as balancing the budget. The resident was more important than the dollar. That's not to say that the good use of the dollar was not important. It's the emphasis that makes the difference. If the emphasis is right, it will filter through to the least of employees.

For the first fifteen years of the Fairhaven ministry, each new employee was personally oriented [usually one on one] by the administrator-chaplain. As the numbers of new employees increased, the orientation was accomplished in groupings of two to six. In these sessions, the Fairhaven philosophy and ideals were explained. Things like these were said: "Every employee at Fairhaven is a person of dignity, no matter how menial a task is performed. Cleaning floors and carrying bedpans are essential tasks for the well-being of residents. Proper handling of garbage, as well as physician care, is needed to maintain good health for a community. So diploma people shall not 'lord it over' those doing menial service. Every person is needed on every level, therefore, give every person his or her 'due' and respect his or her dignity."

Every employee was asked to do at least one thing each day for someone else — doing something that was not a requirement. Thus the employee would have to live, to work, beyond any selfish reasons and would have to think about someone else. This challenge was repeated many times over at employee meetings or at small group seminars or on a one to one basis. People are different when they do things for others. They become altruistically oriented. They become more outgoing. They are not turned inward. There is less selfishness. It makes a better person. It makes a better employee. [This same challenge was give to residents and is discussed in the Chapter "The Residents".]

When people applied for work at Fairhaven, they were never asked if they specifically liked people who were older. The questions always were, "Do you love people? Do you like to be around people?" If the applicant liked to be associated with people, management was convinced that the applicant would be comfortable in the midst of the large Fairhaven family of elderly persons. It never took very long before employees began to love the residents. In one case, a personable young man left Fairhaven employment because the death of resident friends affected him adversely.

Fairhaven administration was always quick to publicly assert that Fairhaven is a home distinctively Christian and church-related. This assertion was not lost on employees. The employees assisted in strengthening the ethical standards and supported the continuance of high moral conduct. Employees openly and affectionately spoke of their own denominational affiliations and how their faith was reflected in the performance of their jobs. The wide range of religious affiliations enhanced the relationship of staff members. In the diversity there was unity.

Honesty and integrity were stressed. Cheating and stealing were not tolerated. There was no excuse for the use of foul language or trash talk. Also, one's word should be one's bond. If a resident's needs could not be met immediately, the resident was to be told why. A time was to be set when the need would be met. Then, at that time, the need should be a priority, regardless how small or unimportant the item may seem to be.

Each employee was asked to give the best of herself or himself and to try to see the best in others. Thus the negative aspects of residents and fellow employees [and sometimes visitors] would be minimized. The best [the positive] would surface and dominate and thus, the family of Fairhaven would be happier.

Another byword: "Tend to the little things! Don't neglect them!" Employees immediately address major problems. That's obvious. Seldom, if ever, are major problems ignored. However, people procrastinate on the little things. It's easy to delay getting the small items addressed. Not getting the little things done becomes annoying to the resident. The squeaky hinge gets squeakier and makes the resident more and more irritable. Whoever thinks little things do not bother, probably has never had a mosquito in the bedroom at night.

Frequent training sessions emphasized these considerations that were designed to help employees be themselves, and more than that, to help them be the best they could be.

In sum, everything reverted to living the Christian faith, to emulate the person and the teachings of Jesus Christ. Residents and employees were continuously conscious that Fairhaven was Christian and church-related. That "rubbed off" on employees.

THE FIRST EMPLOYEE

The Wisconsin Congregational Conference hired the first employee on October 10, 1960 [through Superintendent Jess Norenberg and a search committee] in the person of the Rev. Carroll J. Olm, who was at that time the pastor of St. Paul's Evangelical and Reformed Church [now United Church of Christ], Sheboygan, Wisconsin. He had 13 years of parish ministry experience, including five years as minister at Trinity/St. Luke Evangelical and Reformed Church [now United Church of Christ], Mulberry, Indiana, and five years as minister at Calvary Memorial Evangelical and Reformed Church [now United Church of Christ] in Wauwatosa, Wisconsin. Mr. Olm had no previous employment experience working specifically with the elderly, other than that which the parish ministry afforded.

Jess Norenberg, searching for the future administrator of the projected home, consulted with the Rev. Dr. Al Schmeuzer, the administrator of Evangelical Deaconess Hospital [now Sinai-Samaritan Hospital], Milwaukee. The Evangelical and Reformed Church people had a long history of church-related health and human service involvement. Al Schmeuzer recommended that the Congregationalists consider Carroll Olm, Sheboygan, for the position. When Carroll Olm was serving the Calvary Memorial Evangelical and Reformed Church in Wauwatosa, Deaconess Hospital was interested in him for administrative responsibilities.

Carroll J. Olm—1963
Radke Studio

Subsequently, during the summer of 1960, correspondence was conducted between Jess Norenberg and Carroll Olm. That same summer at the Congregational Pilgrim Camp, Green Lake, Wisconsin, the Rev. Richard Wichlei, assistant superintendent of the Wisconsin Congregational Conference, urged Carroll Olm to seriously consider accepting the challenge to become the first administrator of the future Fairhaven.

The challenge was intriguing; a call was felt; but an inner turmoil developed. The Olms had accepted the call to minister to the congregation of St. Paul's Church in Sheboygan and they only had been serving that parish for not quite two years. Was the call to St. Paul's not an authentic call? If it was authentic, how does one justify leaving that calling to respond to another call? Was the call to go to Whitewater an authentic call? If it was, then one should respond affirmatively, without regrets. How does one know what the will of God is for one's life and ministry? Without having a clear sense of direction, the Olms procrastinated on making the decision.

Finally, the dilemma was resolved. A written listing of nine ministerial goals for St. Paul's Church was discovered. Ironically, all nine goals had not only been addressed, but had been fulfilled.

This was perceived as a message from the Holy Spirit that the call to minister in Whitewater, under the auspices of a different denomination in a special ministry, should be accepted. Completing nine goals was not necessarily the completion of a ministry, but that completing did indicate that a new call could be justified.

It was Mr. Olm's responsibility to hire and organize the rest of the staff. He was directed from conference leadership to establish an initial staff of nine full time employees [excluding himself], with a total salary and wages budget "not to exceed $19,000 per year." Administrator-chaplain Olm and Board Treasurer Clarence Peck promptly discovered that this goal was impossible to achieve. It was impossible to achieve, not only because employees needed fair wages, but also because the large facility could not be operated with only ten employees. After expansions, when Fairhaven was at full strength, a total of 150 employees [full and part time] were on the payroll. Full time equivalency varied around 86. Into the third decade the annual payroll reached over $1,000,000. Over three decades later, it is noteworthy that the first housekeeper was hired at $1.00 per hour, which was considered top wages at that time for that capacity.

One of the problems with the initial acquisition of staff was that there was no budgetary reserve with which to initially begin operations. There was virtually no income when the "home" first opened its doors. During the first month and one-half of operation, only five residents lived in the facility. That did not generate enough income to merit hiring staff. Hence, the administrator-chaplain was the sole employee and did everything, including maintenance, housekeeping, social services, mail delivery, activities, etc.

NELLIE SAUNDERS: HEAD RESIDENT

Miss Nellie Saunders was the first employee hired by Administrator-chaplain Olm. Her employment commenced January 1, 1963. She was engaged as Head Resident for several reasons. First, she intended to become a Fairhaven resident. She would live on the premises and be directly on hand to address immediate problems or needs or issues. Both Buildings D and E were finished when she came, but the apartment Nellie had selected for her retirement [320C] was not ready for occupancy. Hence, she temporarily resided in 101D.

Second, she had experience in the field of serving older persons, having operated a nursing home in her personal residence for considerable years. [This brought balance to the leadership, since the administrator-chaplain had no such experience.]

Third, she was older. At 36 years of age, the administrator-chaplain needed a staff member who had more maturity than he had, who had living experience, and who could identify more personally with the older residents.

Fourth, she was affordable. Nellie had agreed to receive in salary the maximum which Social Security would allow, without imposing significant monetary penalties on those who exceeded that level of income. Since initially there was meager operating income, this arrangement was a "boon" to Fairhaven.

Nellie provided a stability to the first year of living experience at Fairhaven. She was neat, precise, rigid in some respects, personable, courteous and carried, to a degree, an authoritative image. Her intelligence, concern for others, and her knowledge of the Whitewater community and its citizens, proved valuable, indeed. Nellie developed a pride in the Fairhaven ministry and a love for the Fairhaven residents. She was a good fit — the right person, in the right place, at the right time. She lived at Fairhaven until her death.

DOROTHY FULLER: DIRECTOR OF RESIDENTIAL CARE

It was obvious that a full time staff member was needed to augment the good work which Nellie had done in her part time capacity. It was not difficult to hire someone since there was choice. Mrs. Dorothy Fuller, Wonewoc, Wisconsin, was selected. What was more difficult was deciding what title Mrs. Fuller would have. She was to be the main liaison between residents and staff. The job embraced hostess responsibilities, social work, support for activities, counseling, and some public relations work [greeting families and visitors.] There were also tour guide responsibilities. She was to have some initial contact with prospective residents, but the great bulk of that responsibility rested with the administrator-chaplain. The title "Director of Residential Care" was created by the administrator-chaplain and to his knowledge not used anywhere else to that time. It was selected to make certain the traditional titles, steeped in the old folks' homes of yesterday, would never surface. No "superintendent!" No "matron!" There was a breaking away from the old concepts.

Dorothy was suited for her position. She had served as a staff hostess in a large Methodist church in Ashville, North Carolina. She knew how to meet and greet people. She was a smart dresser — an attractive person with magnetic qualities. She gave the program focus and stability. Demonstrating her Christian faith, she proved to be an asset and, at the same time, she was universally well liked. She exemplified in her person the image being fashioned for Fairhaven. The goal was to depict everything at Fairhaven as a class act of top quality. It was to be a dignified, yet warm, personable and loving place. Dorothy emitted this kind of radiance.

WILLIAM MARKHAM AND MILDRED ENLOE: HEAD RESIDENTS

When Nellie Saunders resigned from head resident duties, William Markham, O.D., was engaged to take her place. Dr. Markham brought new dimensions of image to the program. First, he was male. That was different, for the great majority of employees and residents were female. Second, he operated "with" residents, rather than "for" them. He was well dressed and emulated gentleness and politeness. There was little authoritative "air" about him. He was understanding and unassuming. Everyone liked him.

After William Markham died, Miss Mildred Enloe was named Head Resident. Her heart "beat for" Fairhaven and she was delighted to give of herself for the residents and the Fairhaven ministry. She was so dedicated that occasionally she had to be reminded not to work so hard. Mildred was a solid, self-sacrificing employee. Her insights and comments at department head meetings were always helpful and appropriate. She, too, was well liked. In the fourth decade, after Mildred retired from the Head Resident position, she was not replaced by anyone else. Her duties were distributed among other employees in social services, nursing and administration.

BUILDING MANAGERS

A building manager had to be engaged once the first five buildings were completed. About 125 toilettes, 100 plus refrigerators and ranges, boilers, water heaters, water softeners, pumps, radiators, exhaust fans, electric units, pipes, doors, windows, roofs, phones, sewers, etc., all had to be maintained. There was still meager operational income and no reserve from which to draw.

Arthur Harris

A wonderful person by the name of Arthur Harris came on the scene. Art accepted the responsibilities of supervisor of maintenance. He, like Nellie Saunders, worked for what Social Security would allow, without having penalties imposed. Art had spent years farming, so he knew how to fix things. Even though everything was new, he still had plenty to fix.

Art was able to fill all expectations of performance. The extra bonus was his smiling face and jovial manner. He got along beautifully with residents and staff and visitors.

Harold Nelson

Local resident Harold Nelson had retired from farming and school maintenance work. He was employed under the same financial arrangement that was acceptable to Nellie Saunders and Arthur Harris. Harold was another "Art Harris," emulating the same qualities.

Delmar Wendt

Fairhaven needed a full time building manager and found one in Delmar Wendt. Del, much younger than Art and Harold, had also grown up and lived in the rural area. While he had no specific previous employment in building manager capacities, he had a reservoir of knowledge and skill from which to draw. Delmar accepted the full time position with some fear and trepidation. After taking a tour of the facility upon being hired, Del asked seriously, "What do I do when I get lost in these buildings?"

God could not have given us a better person than Del Wendt to be our building manager. He was excellent at his job. He understood the complexities surrounding the rest of the Fairhaven operation. He was faithful and dedicated. He was Christian oriented [a dedicated Lutheran], pleasant to be around, and worked well with others. Residents and employees "loved" him. One day when Del thought a female resident was gone from her apartment, he knelt down in the corridor to fix the kickplate on her exterior door. When he made some noise, the resident who was at home, opened the door to investigate. There was Del on his knees before her, looking up at her. She immediately said, "I accept!"

Delmar grew with Fairhaven, remaining as a cherished member of the staff until his retirement in 1990.

For a limited time Delmar Wendt supervised all maintenance, housekeeping and laundry personnel. Handling all these workers was not Del's "long suit" and he felt the burden of such involvement. A change was made to permit Delmar to focus on his building manager responsibilities and elevate others to the supervision duties.

Franklin Henry, Caroline Hookstead and David Koss

Three likable, industrious, faithful and respected employees, in the persons of Franklin Henry, Caroline Hookstead and David Koss were promoted to housekeeping, maintenance, and laundry supervision. All three demonstrated good organization skills and teaching capabilities. They also demonstrated exceptional rapport with residents and with the employees who worked under them.

DIETITIANS AND FOOD SERVICE SUPERVISORS

Besides housekeeping and maintenance, the first ancillary service that opened was food service. The first meals were served on April 27, 1963.

Dorothy Uhe

Mrs. Dorothy Uhe was the initial food service supervisor and was supported by a staff of cooks, salad makers, bakers, waitresses and dish washers. After she was hired Dorothy asked, "What am I to do?" The answer was, "Prepare quality food in quantity." Dorothy did that. She organized the department well. In the first three decades of Fairhaven food service operation, there were very, very few resident complaints about the food. That was a tribute to Dorothy and her successors. In those three decades, Mrs. Uhe's successors were: Edria DeLisle, Irene Heedrick, Dietitian Constance Hornickel and Dietitian Mary Lynn Mason.

Edria DeLisle and Irene Heedrick

Edria DeLisle and Irene Heedrick were local Whitewater residents who brought hard work, dedication, and love to the program. Edria and Irene did not have food service special training, but they earned stature as certified Food Service Coordinators by successfully completing special vocational training. They worked well with department employees and were able to achieve the food service goals as outlined. Both cooperated well and had excellent rapport with residents.

Dietitian Constance Hornickel

Constance Hornickel was the first full time dietitian on staff. She was the personification of cleanliness and neatness. Her unbound energy and deep dedication to her profession quickly reflected into positive food service strides. Department head meetings were enlivened by the Hornickel "puns."

Connie was intrigued by Fairhaven's thrust to computerize and she negotiated a working agreement with Baraboo Sysco, our food supplier, to coordinate and integrate the Fairhaven computer program with Baraboo Sysco's program. It provided computerized inventory control, purchasing and ordering, pricing, delivery schedules, etc. Administration encouraged Connie to pursue her computer interest by attending classes and seminars in Madison. Fairhaven's encouragement became Fairhaven's "deficit." After a decade of productive employment, Connie

enrolled as a full time University of Wisconsin - Whitewater student and
earned her master's degree in computer science.

Dietitian Mary Lynn Mason

Mary Lynn Mason, Janesville, succeeded Constance Hornickel. She
brought beauty to the food service program, not only through her personal attractiveness, but also by emphasizing that color and arrangement
of food helped to make it taste better. Mary Lynn also developed many
special food occasions by organizing, for a given day, international cui-
sine. Ethnic heritage or national holidays were emphasized by dining
room decorations, music, dress of employees and residents, etc., along
with a selected country's typical menu. There was a day for Germany
[Octoberfest] or Scandinavia or the Pacific Islands or Independence Day
or whatever. Residents responded with enthusiasm.

DIRECTORS OF NURSING

The nursing department opened May 24, 1963. Skilled nursing was
the service dimension that stabilized the Fairhaven ministry.
Independence was emphasized, but when a resident needed physical
assistance, there was a deep appreciation that high quality professional
help was immediately and continuously on hand, right on the premises.
The Fairhaven service program was designed to care for people from
independent living through residency plus, intermediate care, and skilled
nursing care up to physical or mental hospitalization. This broad spectrum of care developed over a period of time. The opening of the 21 bed
infirmary in May of 1963 was the beginning of the process and tremendously important it was to have high standards and the right sense of
direction.

Dorothy Bell

Dorothy Hull Bell, R.N., provided excellent professional leadership
when she established these standards and this direction. She had nurse
training at Milwaukee Hospital [now Sinai-Samaritan Hospital] and fur-
thered her education in Boston where she specialized in pediatrics. Her
expertise was focused at Mercy Hospital, Janesville, Wisconsin, and in
private duty until May 1963, when she accepted the challenge of being
the first Director of Nursing at Fairhaven. She retired from that position
in 1966 and then continued to serve part time until 1978.

In Dorothy Bell, the phrase "Saints of the Lord" was personified. She
was a person of faith, a person kind and self sufficient, a person who possessed strength of character, a person congenial, helpful, loving, who
planned her life around the needs of others.

Why has the Fairhaven nursing program been of such high quality and looked upon as a standard setter? Why do Fairhaven's registered nurses, licensed practical nurses, nursing assistants, therapists, volunteers and others possess sensitiveness, love and utmost of dedication? Here's why: Because Fairhaven's first Director of Nursing Dorothy Bell set proper policies and implemented high standards. Dorothy Bell demonstrated creative leadership and initiated a continuing care program of exceptional quality, saturated with warm, personal, loving nursing care.

Dorothy Hull Bell—1969

This aura of Christian love was real. Over the years, many tributes were received testifying to it. The following one, hand-written on March 16, 1974, by Arthur Brown, son of the Rev. Arthur Brown, resident, epitomizes them all:

> I have a special regard for the nursing staff in the infirmary. I do not know them all by name. But their unending good cheer, kindness and love for people who are no longer what they once were is a particularly marvelous thing. What a spectacular evidence of Christian life!
>
> There is also the wonder of help and support by staff and residents to the surviving spouse . . . . . in this case, Dad. I am sure he could be in no other environment that could be as helpful.
>
> I do not intend this letter to be mawkish and sentimental — though it may sound that way. The depth of feeling runs pretty deep. My regard for you, your staff, and the residents of Fairhaven is unending. May you all prosper in love.

Dorothy's long hours of service and astute judgment won the admiration of her professional colleagues. Her warmth of personality, her reverence for life, her humility in daily contacts should never be forgotten. Dorothy Bell received the Honor Award for Meritorious Service in 1969.

SUCCESSOR DIRECTORS OF NURSING

The "Queen of the Infirmary" died on March 14,1991. Her first three decade successors were: Alicia Hawley, Bernadette Biladou, Barbara Thayer, Lillian Cahill, and Olive Crawley. Kathleen Church Pastor, long time employee, who developed in her nursing career at Fairhaven during the first three decades, was promoted to Director of Nursing in the fourth decade.

All of the successor directors of nursing made their contributions, building on the foundations laid by Dorothy Bell.

Lillian Cahill and Olive Crawley

Both Lillian Cahill and Olive Crawley, through their lengths of service and through their loving hearts, helped to fashion excellence in the program. Both were extremely patient oriented. Lillian Cahill wanted as little to do with administration duties as possible. It was the patient who mattered, regardless of the cost. At the time Olive Crawley was engaged, the administrator-chaplain had "scoured" the state in an attempt to find a Roman Catholic nun, who would be qualified and willing to join the Fairhaven ministry program. He had nuns assisting in the effort to find such a person. The administrator-chaplain deeply appreciated the love and care quality demonstrated by sisters of the orders. He was convinced the acquisition of a nun would be a tremendous asset to the staff. While there was a considerable number of highly qualified applicants for the opening, no nun was among them.

The final choice was Olive Crawley, R.N., Palmyra, Wisconsin, a devout Roman Catholic, who had two siblings who were Roman Catholic nuns. Olive brought all the dimensions of qualifications that the administrator-chaplain was looking for and she contributed unusual dedication and skill to the very demanding position. She was called "our quasi nun!" — and she seemed to revel in it!

Over the decades, the nursing department expanded until all of Building C second floor was skilled nursing. All of Building C third floor was devoted to intermediate care. Most of Building C fourth floor was designated for maximum C.B.R.F. service, which was affectionately titled "Residency Plus."

DIRECTORS OF ACTIVITIES

Great emphasis was placed on resident activities throughout the facility. Floor space was allocated for an activity location, only to be re-allocated later for a different activity. Residents' needs changed constantly, yea, the residents themselves changed. Hence, there was continuous effort to design activities to meet the current needs.

The nine initial lounges provided adequate space for doing things. Then, there were the thousands of square feet in the lower level: library, conference room, beauty shop, carpentry shop, weaving, ceramics, photography, dart ball, billiards and the indoor garden. In 1970, the construction of fellowship hall provided an additional dimension for music, lectures, programs, dramas, banquets, dancing, parties, etc., etc.

Loa Hill, O. T. R. and Wendy Lucht, C. T. R. S.

To organize and maintain all of these diversified and numerous activities, the activities department was created. Mrs. Loa Hill, Occupational Therapist Registered, was chosen to be the first department head. Loa was skilled at her job. In addition to the on-going recreational activities for the residentially self sufficient, she was directed to develop a quality activities/occupational therapy program. Special attention was to be given to the semi-ambulatory and non-ambulatory residents, who predominantly resided in skilled nursing. Respected throughout the state in occupational therapy circles, Loa, with her staff, successfully did just that. Insufficient time and help made it impossible to be all things to all people, but a significant program it was. When Wendy Lucht, C.T.R.S., was engaged, the skilled nursing patient activities programming intensified. Later, Wendy became the worthy successor of Loa Hill.

DIRECTORS OF SOCIAL SERVICE

It took a long time to initiate and develop the Social Services Department, but when it was operable, there was enhancement of programming for the residency.

Ann Ahlman, S. W.

Ann Ahlman, S.W., was the first licensed social worker on the staff. She started everything from scratch. Residents and other employees needed to learn what a social services department did — what the parameters were. Forms had to be created. The whole system of operation and documentation had to be implemented. Referral files were expanded. Coordination had to be developed between health and social programs throughout the city, county and state. Ann used her pleasant manner as an asset to build confidence in the program. She taught everyone about the methods of good social service and she flowed well with the rest of the staff.

Valerie Cole and Kay Demler

Valerie Cole, C.A.P.S.W., and Kay Demler, C.S.W., followed, continuing the good work initially established. These two highly regarded professionals have led the department to new heights of effectiveness and accomplishment.

ADMINISTRATION

While administration was controlling the entire operation from the beginning, the administrative offices were the last to be structurally completed. Administration was governed from the basement of the parsonage at 244 N. Park Street, where the administrator-chaplain had a desk and a typewriter, but no staff. When he was at his desk during the winter season, he had to wear an overcoat and a pair of overshoes to keep warm. After June 1, 1963, when the administration offices opened, operations became more efficient. Residents had not complained. However, now that there were on premise offices, staffed with personnel, life became easier for the residents.

Margaret Winch and Ella Brigham

Organization of the business aspect of a large operation like Fairhaven was no small task. Two older persons, known to each other, both holding commercial degrees from Whitewater Normal School [now University of Wisconsin - Whitewater], both former teachers, both living in Whitewater, were engaged to address the task. Miss Margaret L. Winch was hired as office manager and Mrs. Ella Brigham as office secretary. Margaret was special. She was intelligent, personable, dedicated, had excellent job skills, had a strong moral code, and possessed ability to organize the business affairs. She received help in setting up the financial books from nationally known Professor Paul Carlson of Whitewater State College [now University of Wisconsin - Whitewater] business department. He donated his time and later became a Fairhaven resident. Board Member E.R. Klassy, Fort Atkinson, Wisconsin, was also extremely helpful to Miss Winch as she fashioned the systems for financially controlling Fairhaven.

Ella Brigham and Margaret Winch worked well together. Together they developed all the office procedures for meeting resident needs — everything from mail distribution, to daily announcements, to selling stamps, to answering inquiries and making referrals. They did a fine job.

Miss Winch remained on the job for ten years and then retired. She later became a resident of Fairhaven.

Doris Germundson

The administrator-chaplain selected Mrs. Doris Germundson, Whitewater, to succeed Margaret Winch.. The position provided opportunities for operational innovation and improvement, for after ten years, Fairhaven had developed into a stronger, self-sufficient, more stable enterprise. The methods of office operation that were used over the first ten years now needed to be revised, upgraded, streamlined, and eventually computerized. Doris Germundson was the right person to accept this challenge. She had experience as a small grocery store owner and operator, at Fiberesin Plastics Company, Oconomowoc, and as the office manager of a retail office supply store in Whitewater. She was given the job over several other worthy candidates, partially because she possessed good common sense, because she had good communica-

Doris Germundson
Olan Mills

tion skills, and because she possessed capacities for cooperation, development and growth. This appraisal of her capabilities proved accurate. After learning the theology, philosophy and concepts of the Fairhaven ministry, she integrated them in her employee functions. In addition, she really believed in what the Fairhaven ministry was trying to accomplish. This made her an exceptional employee asset whose working relationship with the administrator-chaplain was an excellent one. After learning how and why Fairhaven functioned the way it did, her evaluation and recommendations were based on those tenets. Hence, she knew how the administrator-chaplain would react to any given issue, based largely on the fundamental concepts that provided the measuring instrument by which judgment was made. There was a bond created which established the guideline for all employees to observe and follow. We called it "smooth working flow." Doris earned her promotion to assistant administrator in 1972 when the Board of Directors authorized the administrator-chaplain to engage a qualified person to assist him in the continuously increasing demands of administration. The directors were surprised when Doris was chosen for the position, for there had been authorization for selecting anyone across the country. The administrator-chaplain suggested, "You know what you have got, but you do not know what you might get." In 1991, shortly after Executive Director Olm retired, she was named administrator, another deserving advancement.

Over the years, Doris Germundson was the glue that held much of the Fairhaven operation together. Her exceptional leadership qualities and her efficient administrative functions on myriad of levels rank her at the pinnacle of performance in the name of Jesus Christ, within the Fairhaven ministry. Her Fairhaven career left an imprint on the ministry that should forever be revered and cherished.

Shirley Hansen

When Doris Germundson was promoted to assistant administrator, Shirley Hansen succeeded her as office manager. Shirley was ethically sound, a Christian advocate [membership with Faith Community Church, Fort Atkinson,] a soft spoken leader who dedicated her heart and life to making Fairhaven what we said it should be.

During the second and third decades of Fairhaven's operational history, Doris and Shirley were a good team. Bookkeeping records were modernized and payroll accounting was streamlined. Budgetary process was upgraded, policies and job descriptions and manuals were re-written. Purchasing was organizationally improved, good inventory control and preventative maintenance schedules were implemented, and reporting and documentation were thorough. The entire facility was computerized. Fairhaven became an efficient, smooth running home.

Doris and Shirley were supported by talented office workers. Two [Linda Koenitzer Peterson and Kathleen Bolchen] were elevated to management positions in the fourth decade.

NON-DEPARTMENT HEAD EMPLOYEES

Those who worked in leadership capacities under the administrator-chaplain have been "lifted up" in the above paragraphs. Each person is deserving. However, let it be quickly proclaimed that the life blood of the Fairhaven staff was not only supplied by the leaders. The regular, in the ranks, employees were genuinely effective. As these pages are being written, the memories of dozens of employees and their excellent contributions are envisioned. There simply is not sufficient space or time to "lift up" each one individually. To be certain, they helped to make Fairhaven what it is. They are God's precious gift to the Fairhaven ministry. Thanks to each one of them!

LONGEVITY

Fairhaven always prided itself on the service longevity of employees. It was not uncommon for a department head to be employed at Fairhaven for 10, 15, 20 years. This longevity brought continuity and stability. It made the total operation easier. It was not that these long time employees could not have gotten other jobs, some at higher wages. They were "sold" on the ministry, feeling the inner satisfactions of service to, for and with God's older children. They did not leave. A real sense of camaraderie matured — a sense of belonging to the Fairhaven family, where we all "lifted" each other up and bore each other's burdens. These quality professionals were always told that if they decided to leave Fairhaven employment for more dollars somewhere else, that words of commendation for service well done would be forthcoming from the administrator-chaplain. They opted to stay. For that we thank them and we praise God!

STAFF CONSULTANTS

If Fairhaven was to reach its goal of ministering to the whole person with quality service, it was necessary to have the best available certified [licensed] professionals for consultation. State law required facilities to engage consultants, thereby trying to ensure full service quality through development of policies and through implementation of policies.

Fortunately, the consultants utilized had long tenures with Fairhaven. They performed in high professional manner and they provided excellent assistance to staff. Having good consultants tended to provide confidence for department heads.

The following served:

Robert Koenitzer, D.D.S., Whitewater, consulting dentist;

Jean Heindel, A.R.T., Fort Atkinson, consulting medical records administrator;

Gary Kilby, D.P.M., Janesville, and Victor Soderstrom, D.P.M., Fort Atkinson, consulting podiatrists;

James Underwood, R.P., Whitewater, and Robert McCullough, R.P., Whitewater, consulting pharmacists;

Ralph Navarre, A.C.S.W., Madison, consulting social worker;

William Cheverette, Whitewater, consulting audiologist;

Richard D. Jentoft, Whitewater, consulting speech therapist;

William Morgan, R.P.T., consulting physical therapist through provider agreement with Fort Atkinson Memorial Hospital [Now Fort Atkinson Memorial Health Services].

MEDICAL DIRECTORS

S. H. Ambrose, M.D., Whitewater;
L.F. Nelson, M.D., Whitewater;
Whitewater Family Practice, Whitewater
  Anne E. Griffiths, M.D.
  Kenneth Kidd, M.D.
  Mark Dickmeyer, M.D.
  Jackie Yaeger, M.D.

Dr. Stephen Ambrose was the initial medical director and served in that capacity from the opening of the skilled nursing section until his death on March 21, 1981. This soft spoken Congregationalist refused compensation for doing the medical director duties. He faithfully and effectively fulfilled his responsibilities and cared for his many patients in skilled nursing.

Dr. L.F. Nelson, a Congregationalist, succeeded Dr. Ambrose as medical director and remained in that capacity until his retirement in 1991. Dr. Nelson served without compensation, until Fairhaven insisted that a mutually agreed stipend be established.

RECRUITING PHYSICIANS

It was obvious that the Whitewater community needed additional medical doctors. Fairhaven administration was deeply concerned in regard to the future availability of medical care. This matter was addressed by Fairhaven hosting a special meeting of key Whitewater people to focus on the issue. An attempt was made to seek solutions to what appeared to be a serious problem. As a result of that meeting, the City of Whitewater appointed a Whitewater Medical Commission, designed to address the need for health care professionals and other health service issues of the city.

The administrator-chaplain also discussed the medical care service projected dilemma with Dr. L.F. Nelson, who verbally assured the administrator-chaplain that he would never let Fairhaven be without medical care. That assurance meant a great deal to administration.

It seemed little was being done to attract physicians to Whitewater. [At least there were no signs of success.] Hence, the administrator-chaplain visited the Wisconsin Medical College and the Deaconess Hospital [now Sinai-Samaritan Hospital] Medical School, Milwaukee. He consulted with the Deans of the schools and with medical school students who would soon become doctors of medicine. As a result, two soon-to-be physicians were entertained and escorted around Whitewater. One of the students stated he was ready and willing to establish his practice in Whitewater after he was licensed. It was a joyous realization. Whitewater was soon to have another physician. However, our "new doctor" missed passing the State Medical examination by one point. Since he was unwilling to wait another year to retake the exam, he was lost to Wisconsin. He took the state boards in Iowa, passed, and established practice in that state.

Continuing efforts to recruit physicians produced nothing. Then the Fort Atkinson Memorial Hospital board, medical staff and administration put their strength to physician acquisition for Whitewater. Strategy meetings were held at the hospital. The administrator-chaplain, along with hospital representatives, wrote letters in behalf of efforts to bring Anne E. Griffiths, M.D., and Elizabeth Tonn, M.D., to Whitewater. There was great satisfaction and rejoicing when both physicians arrived and began giving medical care.

After Dr. Tonn left Whitewater for Minnesota, the administrator-chaplain again supported the hospital's thrust for Whitewater physician recruitment. This time it was to "clear the way" for Dr. Kenneth Kidd to join Dr. Griffiths at the Whitewater Family Practice Clinic. Later Drs. Mark Dickmeyer and Jackie Yaeger joined the clinic.

The physicians at Whitewater Family Practice Clinic shared the medical director responsibilities after Dr. Nelson's retirement from practice. Continued excellent medical consultation was offered and the once projected physician service dilemma was resolved.

MEDICAL DOCTORS ON THE BOARD OF DIRECTORS

During the first three decades, the Board of Directors always tried to have one medical doctor as a member of the board. Those physicians who shared this involvement were: Dr. Carl Newpert, who was Wisconsin's Chief Health Officer, Madison; Dr. Robert B. Ainslie, Madison; Dr. E. Paul Gander, Burlington; Dr. William P. Wendt, Elm Grove; Dr. Louis Nowack, Watertown; and Dr. Ralph L. Suechting, Appleton.

For many years Dr. E. Paul Gander, member of Plymouth Congregational Church [now United Church of Christ,] Burlington, came to Fairhaven once per month to give resident medical examinations. He did this service gratis. Dr. Gander was revered by residents and staff. Attempts to encourage him to move his practice to Whitewater failed.

VOLUNTEERS

In the first three decades, 216,891 volunteer service hours were recorded. These volunteers worked in areas described as: activities, coffee cart, drivers, indoor garden, library, receptionists, special [miscellaneous category covering many services,] and tour guides.

Each spring a volunteer recognition luncheon was held to treat and honor the volunteer workers. Special recognition was given to those who recorded accumulated hours totaling 100, 250, 500, 1000, and every 500 additional hours after 1000 hours [1500, 2000, 2500, etc.]

At the end of 1989, Resident Edith DeMoulpied was the top volunteer with 9000 hours of service.

THE OLM FAMILY

Marilyn G. Olm, wife of the administrator-chaplain, and the three Olm children [Mark, Elizabeth Ann and James] served in a voluntary, supportive capacity. From the very beginning, the residents and employees of Fairhaven were embraced as an extended part of the Olm family.

The residents were loved by Marilyn and the children. This was greatly appreciated by residents and a strong bond of affection was cre-

The Olm Family—1965 L-R: Mark, Marilyn, James, Carroll and Elizabeth Ann.

ated. No children had more quasi grandparents than did the Olm children. The children were easy to love because they were friendly, affectionate and well behaved. They knew where disciplinary limits were. On one occasion, when Jimmy was about six years old, he was at Fairhaven with one of his friends. They were dropping a small rubber ball between the stairways from the fourth floor of Building C to the basement. A resident told him not to do that. Jimmy responded, "Oh, it's all right for us to do this, my daddy owns Fairhaven." Residents often commented how wonderful it was to watch the children grow and mature.

There was also warmth developed between the employees and the Olm family. Friendliness prevailed again. Genuine, down to earth affection, was extended to employees. They, in turn, quickly embraced the family as part of the employee family.

The children were taught that they represented Fairhaven as much as anyone else, hence, they were supposed to be on their good behavior. They knew that if they did anything improper, it would be a reflection, not only on the Olm family, but on all those good, wonderful people at Fairhaven. Their proper conduct, friendliness, politeness, smiles and their willingness to do something for another without compensation, just for the joy such service gives, contributed to Fairhaven's positive image.

The parsonage was open to board members, residents and employees. Board members from greater geographic distances were lodged and "broke bread." Residents and employees respected the need for privacy, but "pop-in" visits occurred, undoubtedly because the parsonage was in such close proximity to Fairhaven.

Marilyn held Open House for residents, partly because the residents would know us better if they knew where and how we lived. Open Houses for residents were held even after 63 new apartments were added when Building AA was constructed. From that time on, Open House was held two full days — mornings and afternoons — so all residents could be accommodated. The dining room table was laden with treats.

The family agreed to participate in Fairhaven events, such as programs, services, holidays, celebrations. In so doing, Olm quality family time was sacrificed. For instance, on Christmas eve an elegant Christmas banquet dinner was served gratis to residents. On Christmas Eve employees wanted to be with their families. To accommodate employees, the administrator-chaplain and some of the department heads, came with their children to Fairhaven to serve the banquet. It was unique, different, to be sure, but genuinely appreciated by the residency. Late Christmas eve [after 11:00 p.m.] the Olm children would go to every apartment door and slip a Christmas morning message from the administrator-chaplain, staff and board of directors under it. It took 45 minutes to accomplish this task. Then on the next morning — every Christmas morning for three decades — the Olm family joined the administrator-chaplain for the resident Christmas morning "family" get-to-gether. It was the sharing of the joys of the day, joke telling, some caroling with Mrs. Olm at the piano, story telling, recitation of poems, reflections on Christmas' past, distribution of fruit. The Olm children performed — specially with instruments and singing. In the third decade, the Olm grandchildren also were involved on Christmas morning. Leah Olm [from Duluth], Jim and Bitsy's daughter, at three years old, danced and sang — yes, sparkled — for residents. A real hit!

It became a tradition to have the Christmas morning festivities end with the attending residency singing, "Silent Night, Holy Night." Everyone stood in a circle holding hands, surrounding fellowship hall. The only lighting came from the colorful Christmas tree. An emotionally moving experience!

Then the Olm family would lead a caroling for another hour in the infirmary [skilled nursing section]. Several residents joined them and at least one carol was sung in each skilled nursing room. Fruit was distributed. Tears at times, yes! Precious moments!

It was then past noon on Christmas day and the Olm children ran home, because now their personal family Christmas could be celebrated.

The intent and goal was to make the Christmas celebration at Fairhaven so intimate, pleasant and enriching that residents, who were fortunate enough to be with families, would return to Fairhaven with less to share than those who stayed at Fairhaven for Christmas. Christmas at Fairhaven became so exciting, popular and spiritually satisfying that some residents, when invited to join their family Christmas celebration in subsequent years, declined to do so saying, "I/we want to be here. If we leave, we'll miss too much. I/we will come to your house another time."

TOUCHE' — Mission accomplished!

Similar sacrifice was made for three decades of Thanksgiving Day celebration. Father always conducted Thanksgiving Day worship service at Fairhaven on Thanksgiving morning, before the family could travel to relatives for celebrating their personal Thanksgivings.

Then, the Independence Day parade or Memorial Day, whatever — Fairhaven received the priority.

Sometimes the children complained, "Why must we always do this?" After dad's retirement, it was heart warming to hear them say that they truly missed the involvement at Fairhaven over Christmas. "It just does not seem right — it's not the same!" Patterns were not easily broken after three decades.

The family was constantly affected by emergency calls. This was especially true in the first decade and one-half, when the children were smaller. The phone would ring and dad would have to leave because something was wrong at Fairhaven or someone needed him in some way — day and night!

It became a laughing matter when the family would be returning from a vacation trip and immediately — and that means within one minute — the phone would ring because father would be wanted at Fairhaven. Mother often laughingly said, "They can smell it when dad gets home."

Credit must be given to the family for graciously accepting that father had to work long, hard hours for the ministry most days of the month. It had to be done if Fairhaven were to succeed. In the early years there was no one else to do it. No excuses — others work many days and long hours, too — but the family did sacrifice quality time with father for the sake of the ministry.

In the parish, the minister can leave the church after Labor Day Sunday, for instance, and usually not be bothered in any way until Tuesday morning, a day and one-half later. It was not so for Fairhaven's administrator-chaplain. Fairhaven cared for residents 365 days a year, 24 hours a day. Nothing ever closed down or reduced in intensity. It never ended. Even after the engagement of an assistant administrator, the emergency demands lessened only in small part.

During the "absent father" days, mother carried the family load. In addition, she was always a positive asset for Fairhaven promotion. She requested that Fairhaven affairs not be discussed at home. That request was respected and, hence, she was sheltered from most of the stress and strain of administration. She could honestly say she did not know, when questions were asked her about Fairhaven operations. That was advantageous.

Marilyn always was a source of inspiration and made the administrative functioning easier because she was [and is] a loving and devoted spouse, who was both father and mother on too many occasions. The happiness in home environment — a loving and supportive spouse — helped to make whatever success was achieved. So often, a person who is happy in home life, will be successful in the work-a-day world.

Two years after former Conference Superintendent Jess Norenberg retired he wrote,

> It seems you are helped much by your family. Marilyn fits
> into the picture perfectly and even the children seem thoroughly
> at home. What a blessing to you, to Fairhaven, and to us all. Both

Arthur Brown and Phil Day spoke of this. [Note: Arthur Brown, a Congregational minister, retired in Whitewater and later, with his spouse, became a resident. Phil Day, at the time, was minister of Congregational Church [now United Church of Christ], Whitewater.]

On March 12, 1969, Director of Nursing Dorothy Bell wrote the following, when she was notified that she was to be a recipient of the Honor Award for Meritorious Service:

> I am grateful for this award and honor, but I am more grateful for the support, understanding and friendship of the last six years. And like all the rest of the 140 grandmothers in Fairhaven, I really feel that you and Marilyn and company belong to me.

Another testimony to the family's involvement in the life of Fairhaven was penned on September 17, 1976, by Helen Daggett of Whitewater, who later with her husband, Clay, became a resident:

> . . . We just want to express our appreciation of you, Marilyn and your children and marvel how our community, church and lives have been enriched by the whole Olm family.

After 15 years or so in the throes of the Fairhaven ministry, Marilyn was named "Mrs. Wonderful" by her husband. She is lovingly known by that name throughout the United States and even in Germany, where they call her "Frau Wunderbar!" It is an affectionate deserving title.

CHAPTER XI

Church - Relatedness

"The love of Christ [compels] us. . . ."
II Corinthians 5:14 KJV

[Note: A portion of this chapter is cited from an address given by the author at the 1987 annual meeting of the Wisconsin Conference of theUnited Church of Christ, Appleton, Wisconsin. Special thanks and acknowledgment is given to the Rev. Dr. Frederick R. Trost, president of the Wisconsin Conference, who offered editing and advice for that presentation.]

Sometimes giving birth is easier than other times. Parents come in a variety of sizes and shapes, with differences of age, experience, emotions, strengths and weaknesses. Then too, the size of the "baby" can determine the amount of pain known. Perhaps it is fair to say that the amount of travail endured and/or the amount of joy experienced is relative. Each birth being uniquely its own.

Historically, this observation is verified in the life of the church as Christian faith "brought into the world" a myriad of health and human service facilities, dedicated to providing direct care and healing for God's children. Each such "birth" is uniquely its own, too. The motivation for this "parenting" is rooted in both the Scriptures and early Christian community life.

Shortly after the Rev. Dr. Frederick R. Trost became the president of the Wisconsin Conference of the United Church of Christ, he related what happened when Bensenville Home Society [now Lifelink, Inc.,] Bensenville, Illinois, officials razed the old castle building, which for years had housed older people from the Chicago area. When they opened the cornerstone box, among other things, they found a simple sentence written in the German language. It said, "The love of Christ [compels] us!" [II Corinthians 5:14 KJV.]

In health and human service ministries, as in other things we do, "The love of Christ compels us!" [II Corinthians 5:14 KJV.] Why? Because Christians have heard the Gospel — the good news of salvation — that God is in action saving the world through Jesus Christ, the Son. Christians have heard the preaching of that Gospel. In the New

Testament Greek it is called kerygma. Those who heard that Word of God were bound by the power of the Holy Spirit into what the New Testament Greek calls koinonia, the congregation, the fellowship of believers, the communion of saints.

The faith generated in *koinonia* — in the believers — found expression in two main ways. The first was in *didache*, the teaching; and that is why Christians still emphasize Sunday church schools, catechism classes, vacation Bible schools, and church-related academies, colleges and seminaries. Second, *diakonia* surfaced and became dominant in early Christian history. *Diakonia* literally means "service." It comes from *diakonos*, a servant, one who waits on tables. Here emerged the concept of "bearing one another's burdens." As a demonstration of their faith, Christians literally "had to — were compelled to — give the cup of cold water in the name of the Lord." [Matthew 10:42.]

The admonitions of the Christ set forth clearly the church's mission and responsibility:

> Go about peacemaking.
> Do justice.
> Feed the hungry.
> Heal the sick.
> Visit those in prison.
> Support the oppressed.
> Comfort the widow in her affliction.

The United Church of Christ Statement of Faith, as adapted by Robert V. Moss, says, "God calls us into the Church. . .to be servants in the service of the whole human family. . ."

Health and human service ministries are an embodiment of Christ's presence in our midst. In Matthew 25:40 [KJV] Jesus says, "Inasmuch as you have done it unto one of the least of these. . . . .you have done it unto me." In other words, the ministry is to the Lord's own self. May it not be the Lord who is the prisoner, the poor, the hospital intensive-care patient, the battered child, the alcoholic, the widower, the long-term care person who has lost good judgment? This is not to deal in the abstract, for the church is called to face the daily sufferings of humankind, and we find our crucified Lord personified in those sufferings.

Jesus, on his earthly pilgrimage, showed us the way. Yes, He preached! Yes, He taught! Equally, He ministered *diakonia!* Jesus is **Servant**! "The Son of Man came not to be ministered unto, but to minister." [Matthew 20:28 KJV.] Try to enumerate all the healing miracles. Read the Gospel according to Luke and realize what a dominant part of Christ's ministry is *diakonia*. He went about doing good. He brought about "wholeness" to humanity. He manifested, cultivated, and bestowed *shalom*, that peace which passes understanding. Already in the Old Testament book of Jeremiah [Jeremiah 30:17 KJV.] we hear:

> I will restore health [to you,]
> And I will heal [you] of [your] wounds, [says] the Lord.

"Comfort ye, comfort ye my people, says the Lord!" [Isaiah 40:1.] Comfort, compassion, love! Where there is comfort, where there is compassion, where love abounds, hope continues to grow. That's what *diakonia* is all about. The love of Christ compels us so that God's people may hope. With that hope comes wholeness, *shalom*. Health, healing, and salvation come from God. Christ is powerfully at work as laity and ordained persons live their faith with joy.

We see this powerful, yet tender presence of Christ, exemplified in health and human service ministries. It gives all of us reason to be glad and to be thankful. Health and human service ministries are not an after thought, a postscript; they are at the heart of the matter. These ministries are the church. A visitor at Fairhaven exclaimed, "Here is the body and blood of Jesus Christ; here are people bearing one another's burdens in the love of Christ."

We are grateful for our Christian heritage and for the love and commitment of a servant church. In the varied work of the health and human service ministries, the love of Christ is compelling us.

The church and the facility are ". . . . .one in the Spirit and one in the Lord." They live together in partnership, in covenant, in trust. Each member institution of the health and human service ministries exists legally as a separate corporation, yet together they represent the symbolic arms and hands of believers carrying out the mission. There is self-determination within this covenant circle, yet the theological heritage of the church permeates.

The Wisconsin Conference of the United Church of Christ elects members to the boards of directors of these ministries. Those boards — primarily composed of Wisconsin Conference members in good and regular standing — set the policies under which the diakonic services operate. Perhaps the best way to describe the relationship is, indeed, to say they are in covenant with God and with each other. Nourished by the Gospel message, they recognize mutual goals, purposes and objectives. They are partners in the mission of the United Church of Christ. The conference upholds its part of the covenant by giving guidance, consultation, fiscal oversight, theological relevance and thoughtful, prayerful support

of these ministries. The beloved late professor Elmer Arndt of Eden
Theological Seminary, Webster Groves, Missouri, spoke of it this way:

> The case for church-related health and [human service]
> agencies does not rest solely on the desirability of providing an
> alternative to the services of public agencies. No doubt the pro-
> vision for a choice is good. But our commitment is to something
> more ultimate than the principle of pluralism.
>
> The case rests firmly upon the dual conviction that social
> welfare is not only an essential part of the church's total ministry,
> but it finds its greatest fulfillment in its commitment to that
> church.
>
> To accept such an understanding of the church-related
> health and [human service] agencies is to accept serious respon-
> sibilities. It means for one thing that the church will insist on the
> highest standards of professional training and competence for
> those engaged in its diakonal work. It means that the church will
> accept the responsibility for providing the means so that its min-
> istry in social welfare may be done well. It means that the church
> will regard the work of its health and [human service] ministries
> as an integral part of its mission in the world. It means that the
> church will accept, as its responsibility, the task of uniting the
> prophetic call to righteousness with the work of compassion, of
> uniting the concern for [a person's] welfare on earth with con-
> cern for his [or her] eternal destiny, and of uniting the power of
> the new life in Christ with new knowledge and skills devoted to
> the service of [others]. *1

Faith demands a certain kind of abandonment. Faithful preaching
demands relevant relationship to society. In this we are in partnership, in
covenant. Health and human service ministries are, of course, account-
able for partnership, for quality of service, for fiscal efficiency and for
charity. Where *diakonia* is alive, it is anchored in the life in Christ. There
is an emphasis on ministering to the whole person — physical, mental,
emotional, spiritual. The beauty or extent of our facilities does not make
a ministry. Where *diakonia* lives, the Word has become flesh. Love is put
into care. It must be unashamedly spiritual.

1* From an address delivered to the membership of the Council for
Health and Human Service Ministries of the United Church of Christ,
later printed and distributed to the membership.

The love of Christ compels us — to do what? And how? Since the basic arena of Christian service is the local congregation, the what and how were traditionally centered in a local church or in a smaller group of local churches, allowing the love of Christ to inspire to *diakonia*. A local church sees need and establishes a diaconial service for the elderly. [i.e. - The Church of the Beatitudes, formerly Congregational, now United Church of Christ, Phoenix, Arizona, founds "The Beatitudes," a retirement community for the aging.] A group of congregations organize a Deaconess Society or a Benevolent Society and the society sponsors a facility [i.e. - The Evangelical Deaconess Society, formerly Evangelical and Reformed, now United Church of Christ, St. Louis, Missouri, established the Deaconess Hospital, St. Louis.]

In Fairhaven's case, it was not a local church or a society or a limited number of committed congregations that banded together. In Fairhaven's case, from the very beginning, it was "the conference," all of the congregations of the Wisconsin Congregational Conference [now Wisconsin Conference United Church of Christ] who sponsored the program. This basic structure design — which committed the entire conference to the Fairhaven ministry — was physically symbolized in at least four ways:

[1] Initially the conference provided direct and controlling leadership.

[2] The conference itself co-signed the first mortgage and became financially liable for the Fairhaven operation.

[3] The conference minister was declared an ex officio member of the Fairhaven Board of Directors.

[4] The conference churches committed to a significant fund raising effort.

The church-relatedness of Fairhaven is reflected in several ways [as is true of almost all, if not all, church sponsored facilities:]

[1] The Mission Statement. The objective for being is legally defined. Usually it is very broad in scope so that the facility would not be too closely restricted in its mission should times and needs demand a broader spectrum of service. Changing times demand changing responses.

[2] The operation is strictly not-for-profit. This characteristic is not universal in church-related situations, for some church-related facilities are operated **for**-profit. For-profit operations are subject to paying all tax obligations. In a not-for-profit facility, no pecuniary profit may be realized by any person or group.

Whatever income is produced must be used only for the mission [ministry] as defined in the Articles of Incorporation and Bylaws. For example: No monetary gain or payment of any kind is made to members of the board of directors. Only when board members drove hundreds of miles for Fairhaven were traveling expenses reimbursed. Only employees received compensation.

[3] The Articles of Incorporation and Bylaws require a reversionary clause that guarantees that if ever and whenever the mission [ministry] would cease, all assets that remain after the cessation of operation would revert to a not-for-profit organization. [In Fairhaven's case, that organization is the Wisconsin Conference of the United Church of Christ and then, the assets may be used only for services as described in the purpose for the organization's — Fairhaven's — existence.]

[4] Charity shall be done. Those less fortunate in the world shall be recipients of the organization's benevolence.

Shortly after three decades of Fairhaven's existence, a couple from a neighboring community visited Fairhaven with intent to evaluate whether or not this was the place for their retirement. They were favorably impressed, but felt a need to make comparisons. After visiting another church-related retirement facility, they returned to Fairhaven to confirm that their first impressions were correct. Subsequently, an application was made for future residency at Fairhaven. Sharing their experiences with a relative, this remark was made, "The second facility we visited is business; Fairhaven is ministry."

Both facilities are considered church-related. Yet, for those applicants, the "spirit of ministry" permeated only one of the two places. There is more to church-relatedness than simply sponsorship, if true ministry is to be realized.

For the church to "give birth" to a facility and then to "cut off" significant relationship, exposes opportunity for the facility to emphasize other than Christian values.

If this is true, then in addition to initial church-sponsorship, in addition to meeting all legal requirements for not-for-profit organizations, church-relatedness means a **continuous** demonstration that the ministry is carrying out its defined purpose and is in operational practice — in day by day living — a church-related facility. There should be a continuing permeation of the Holy Spirit. Everything that is done should reflect that the Lord is present and **that** presence is reflected in everything that happens. In other words, not only church-related in word [in structure], but also in deed. It should be reflected in all contacts — with residents, families, visitors, employees, etc. It means caring, reaching out, wherever one can. In every circumstance of life there is a choosing to "bear fruit." That requires one to remain close to the center, for Jesus Christ said, "I am the vine, you are the branches." [John 15:1-8.]

The Apostle Paul wrote, "Pray without ceasing. . . . ." [I Thessalonians 5:17 KJV.] Likewise, in a church-related facility, reflect the Lord's presence without ceasing. The Holy Spirit is among us and, hence, we act not of ourselves. We are different people — we are the **Easter** people — because the risen Lord is with us and controls us, yea, compels us. [See Chapter "The Residents".] Here we have the essence of Christian living: one should not separate day by day living from Christian faith. The Christian religion is not something which is isolated for Sunday morning church service. It is an absorption into day by day living. Hence, once again, Fairhaven is without reservation, church-related, is without being ashamed or embarrassed, Christian [Christ centered.] Fairhaven's operation is not separated from its faith.

For that reason, the board of directors was convinced that the chief executive officer of the corporation should be an ordained minister. That is not to say that a qualified layperson could not do the job. The facility had to be run by an ordained clergyperson with business sense or by a business oriented lay person with a shepherd's heart. The Holy Spirit can permeate through either one of the two. However, the distinction given to the ordained may provide an aura that symbolizes what the church is attempting to accomplish. Linking the title "Administrator" with the title "Chaplain" was further symbolic of that attempt by the church. Here it is visibly: Administrator-chaplain. Religion is combined with life. The administration reflects the faith in which this ministry was conceived, reflects the faith in which this ministry is sustained.

There are those who criticize the blending of the administrative duties with the chaplaincy duties, feeling the chaplaincy role might exist in conflict with administrative functioning. "Keep those separate," they say, "because when rates are raised, or whatever, and the actions of administration are not well received by residents, there will be a barrier to functioning in a pastoral way." Not necessarily so, for administration should be committed to living the faith in all circumstances. Not so, if administration truly abides in the Christian role and always tries to make decisions in the spirit of the Christ. Administration should be coming in love, even when the rates have to be raised, or whatever. Why should "the faith" be left out when the going is tougher? Should that not be the very time when the love of Christ can be best demonstrated?

All of this is not to say that the two functions — administration and chaplaincy — cannot be divided, while retaining the basic "Holy Spirit permeates" concept. It must be recognized, however, that linking administration with chaplaincy in one position does put an extra burden on the individual performing the service.

There were overtures made to administration that a congregation should be established at Fairhaven, with the majority of members being residents. This idea was vigorously opposed by the administrator-chaplain. Fairhaven was not designed to be a congregation. A goal was to integrate the residents into the life stream of the community to the greatest extent possible. Urging residents to retain their denominational affiliation and to become as active as possible in a local church was one way of trying to meet that goal of integration into community life.

Thus, no church services were conducted at Fairhaven on Sunday mornings in conflict with local church services. No funeral services were permitted. The local church pastors should feed the flocks on Sunday mornings and the local church pastors should minister to the families in bereavement.

Fairhaven assisted the local churches in the spiritual development of the local church members who lived at Fairhaven. Vesper services on Sunday evenings at 6:00 p.m. were conducted by visiting church pastors. They also led devotionals at 9:00 a.m. on Thursdays. There were Bible study classes and prayer circles. Immediately after a resident died [preferably within the first five hours] a memorial service celebrated the resident's life. This service was designed to minister to residents and was not intended as a substitute for a family funeral service. By announcing the memorial service, the notice of a resident's death was simultaneously made.

In anticipation of engaging a successor person to follow the Rev. Dr. Olm, at the time of his approaching retirement, the board of directors stood firm in its conviction that an ordained person should be chosen. After a nation-wide search for a clergy person, who had experience in administering a retirement community, failed to produce any acceptable candidate, the administrator chaplain suggested two other methods of searching for the successor. First, to seek a lay person with a shepherd's heart. Second, to seek an ordained person serving in a parish and bringing that person on staff for education and training and internship a year or two years prior to the administrator-chaplain's departure. The board unanimously opted for the latter suggestion and directed Dr. Olm to select three ordained candidates for presentation to the search committee. The board selected the successor, the Rev. David Yochum, Clinton, Iowa, from the three candidates.

Yasu Maruyamano returned to his native Japan after being on the Cedar Lake Home Campus, West Bend, Wisconsin, for three months. Before he left for home, he shared something of his insights. He wrote,

> Because of their religious affiliation, my parents, my aunts, my uncles and my family never told me they like me; never expressed love; never held me or kissed me. You can imagine my state of confusion after arriving on the campus and having, in a very short time, people express kindness to me, and even love. People affectionately taking me into their arms and hugging me.
>
> I, of course, feared having fallen into the hands of a very immoral campus society. But as time went by, the absolute sincerity of the residents and staff came shining through. A new world was unfolding around me. I soon discovered the Spirit behind all of the kindness and generosity was a mankind named Jesus Christ. You cannot [and never will be able to] imagine my deep need response to the likes of real affection and trusting friendships. I began to want to know this Jesus better and how His Spirit teaches people to be kind and loving.
>
> Then I was invited to be a wise man in the campus traditional resident Christmas pageant. Through that experience I learned about the loving parents of Jesus, Mary and Joseph, and how He was born in a stable.
>
> I go to my homeland in Japan with many fine things I have learned and will share. But I shall be very lonely, for you see, in my country there will not be friends who will feel free to hug me or to say "I like." "I love." I plan to learn to know Jesus better and perhaps one day our people, especially our elderly, will accept being told they are loved and will know the joy of hugs and kisses. Thank you for all your patience with me and for teaching me not to be afraid of being a loving, caring person.

Sisters and brothers in the faith! May the love of Christ continue to compel us, "for [entrusted] to us is the ministry of reconciliation!" [II Corinthians 5:18 KJV.]

Epilogue

On June 22, 1989, I gave my final written report on the Fairhaven ministry to the Board of Directors. At that time I did not know that this book, *FAIRHAVEN: GOD'S MIGHTY OAK — [The Development of the Fairhaven Ministry — The First Three Decades]* would be authored by me. But God knew! Through God's inspiration, these several paragraphs concluded one section of that report and now find a fitting place at the conclusion of this VOLUME I:

[Today,] it is absolutely essential that we take time to thank God for blessings bestowed. Don't you feel God's love among us? Christian love is permeating us, lifting us up, drawing us to God in whose name we meet and to whose glory we live and work. All that we are or have has come from God. Even as it is so boldly displayed at the Christian League for the Handicapped here in Walworth County: We are "Blessed to be a Blessing" to others.

The preacher in me forces selection of a Scriptural text for this memorable occasion. The one chosen is recorded in Matthew 13:31,32: "Another parable he [Jesus] put before them saying, The kingdom of heaven is like a grain of mustard seed which a man took and sowed in his field; it is the smallest of all seeds, but when it has grown it is the greatest of all shrubs and *becomes a tree, so that the birds of the air come and make their nests in its branches*1." This is the kingdom of God. A littlest seed — the greatest of shrubs — *a tree with birds in the branches*1. God takes the smallest of beginnings and brings it to mature stature.

Conference President Frederick Trost, Board President Marshall Johnston, Board Secretary-treasurer Fern Fellwock, Pastors Robert Johnston, Robert Kuechmann and Max Rigert, and Director Attorney William J. Willis, and others of you, will vouch for the honored position Fairhaven has in the ranks of the field servicing older people and in the diakonic ministries of the church. That was not always true. Once Fairhaven was a "problem child" and pretty much "small potatoes." Some of us laid awake nights, had bad dreams, wondering from where the money would come. How could this work ever be accomplished?

Listen to words from one of my early sermons: "God, whose love sustains the sparrow on the housetop and the flower in the

*1 Italics added.

165

meadows, will surely sustain us. God, who gave us an only Son, will freely give us all things. With God at our side, there need be no fear for the future. The Lord, whose benediction rested upon our yesterdays, will continue to bless our tomorrows." And truly it is evident that it happened.

God planted a seed — it grew. God watered, God cultivated and suddenly there is a tree. Friends, only God can make a tree. A tree of nature and a tree like Fairhaven, to which I am alluding*1. We get fine compliments about Fairhaven's ministry. We all get them, don't we? But, let that not go to our heads, for, after all is said and done, it's still the Lord who gives the growth. We can put a seed in the ground, but we can't make it grow. God does that!

When we let God's way prevail, great things happen. *The seed becomes a tree*1.* We can't prove that God does that, but we believe it. We believe it because we are Christian and we hear Christ's words: "I am with you always!" This is not something you can argue about very well. You have to say, "Here it is, take it or leave it." And we choose to take it. That's what makes us part of the church. We believe God shows us ourselves in all our bewilderment and sin. Then God shows the God self, something of God power, God love, God justice, God peace — and the call for decision comes — yes or no. God grants a faith, a spirit, a confidence that dictates an acknowledgment of God's granting the increase. *And suddenly, we see the full grown tree *1!*

So, thank you, Lord — thank you for nearly three decades of ministerial privilege.

Can't you hear the words of the oak tree on the front lawn of Fairhaven? —

Fairhaven, you have grown up within our shadows and you, Fairhaven, are so much like us —

You are strong and majestic!
You are lasting and beautiful!
You have survived the snows and the winds!
You are a haven for God's loved ones!

Yes, Fairhaven, God has nurtured us. Through God's grace we have grown from acorns into oaks!

*1 Italics added.